TWENTY-FIRST CENTURY TEACHING GUIDE FOR INDIAN SCHOOLS

SOCIAL SCIENCE BOOK II

Suvraleena Bandyopadhyay is based in Kolkata and is a seasoned teacher and examiner with expertise across international and Indian education boards. She brings the past alive with her dynamic teaching style showing students how the social sciences shape the world we live in today. With years of classroom and assessment experience, Suvraleena continues to be fascinated by the stories History tells, the terrains Geography uncovers, the power of Civics and by the infinite opportunities that the social sciences hold to inspire the future.

PEDAGOGY SERIES

Twenty-First Century

TEACHING GUIDE FOR INDIAN SCHOOLS

Social Science 2

Suvraleena Bandyopadhyay

For Classes 6–8

hachette INDIA

First published in 2025 by Hachette India
(Registered name: Hachette Book Publishing India Pvt. Ltd)
An Hachette UK company
www.hachetteindia.com

1

ISBN: 978-93-5731-584-5

Hachette Book Publishing India Pvt. Ltd
4th & 5th Floors, Corporate Centre,
Plot No. 94, Sector 44, Gurugram 122003, India

Typeset in Adobe Garamond Pro 11.5/16
by Content Respondus
New Delhi

FSC
www.fsc.org
MIX
Paper | Supporting responsible forestry
FSC® C010615

Printed and bound in India
by Thomson Press India Ltd.

Contents

Chapter 1

Knowledge and Ways of Knowing

The ignited mind of the youth is
the most powerful resource
on the earth, above the earth
and under the earth.[1]

Knowledge is often understood in terms of enlightenment. It can be seen as breaking the veil of ignorance and creating awareness in the minds of learners.[2] For Plato, knowledge requires explanation.[3] In Plato's treatment of knowledge, there are three dialogues: *Meno*, *Theaetetus* and *Republic*. David Wolfsdorf explained that in Meno, propositional knowledge is considered a kind of justified true belief. 'If one knows some proposition p then: one believes that p. p is true, and one has some sort of justification for p. For example, I know that the rumbling sound outside my office window is due to a construction worker using a jackhammer (machine) to break up the concrete walkway (path) that leads to my building. I know this because I believe it; it is true and I have justification for my belief. My justification is that I saw the construction worker jackhammering the walkway when I arrived this morning and heard the loud rumbling coming from his work. Plato is often taken to have apprehended this idea or something akin to it…'[4]

Plato's *Theaetetus* is a dialogue devoted to the question of what knowledge (*epistêmê*) is. The narrators recount a conversation that Socrates had the day before his trial with Theodorus of Cyrene, who taught geometry at Athens, and his young student, Theaetetus, who would later go on to make some significant mathematical discoveries. After an introductory discussion about what Socrates is looking for, *Theaetetus* proposes three definitions of knowledge, each of which is subjected to critical examination and then rejected in turn: Knowledge is perception, it is true opinion, or it is true opinion accompanied by a *logos*.[5]

In his *Republic*, Plato compares the usual cognitive condition of human beings to that of prisoners chained in an underground cave, with a great fire behind them and a raised wall in between. The prisoners are chained in position and so are able to see only shadows cast on the facing wall by statues moved along the wall behind them. They take these shadows to be reality. The account of the progress that they would achieve if they were to go above ground and see the real world in the light of the sun features the notion of knowledge as enlightenment.[6]

Theaetetus, along with *Meno* and *Republic*, form the three most significant works to understand Plato's epistemology and theory of knowledge.[7]

Ways of Knowing

A teacher trains and assists learners in the critical evaluation of knowledge so that they can see how different types of knowledge have to be judged in different ways. This allows learners to evaluate new knowledge and understand the relation to specific knowledge issues.[8] There are multiple ways by which learners can be initiated into the process of knowing. Ann Hartman, writing in 'Social Work', January 1990, Vol. 35, No. 1 (January 1990), highlights the importance of multiple ways of knowing:

> 'We must not turn our backs on any opportunities to enhance our knowledge, whether they be examinations of correlations or explications of myths, which, according to Rein and White (1981), align 'rational action with normative ideals and historical commitments', We must attend to the theoretical advances of our scholars and academicians but also gather and listen to the 'stories that rise up out of practice', which 'confront, challenge, confirm, or deny the stories that "come down" from the distal citadels of the profession'. All of these sources are essential to our profession and should enrich the pages of this journal.'[9]

She elaborates on different ways by which learners comprehend knowledge; some might demand distance and objectivity, whereas others rely on deeply personal and empathic knowing. Some will find the validation of their findings through statistical analysis and probability tests, while others will find it through the intensity and authenticity of 'being there' (Geertz, 1988) or through public and shared consensus in what has been called 'practice wisdom' (Siporin, 1989). Some learners also try to predict, whereas others turn to the past for an enhanced understanding of the present.[10]

Keeping this broad spectrum of learners and their favoured conditions of knowing, we will now dive deep into pedagogies and what we mean by social sciences.

Chapter 2

Pedagogies and Learning Theories

> 'We are unknown to ourselves, we men of knowledge – and with good reason. We have never sought ourselves – how could it happen that we should ever *find* ourselves? It has rightly been said: "Where your treasure is, there will your heart be also"; *our* treasure is where the beehives of our knowledge are. We are constantly making for them, being by nature winged creatures and honey-gatherers of the spirit; there is one thing alone we really care about from the heart? – "*bringing something home.*"'
>
> —Friedrich Nietzsche[11]

This quest of 'honey-gatherers' for the 'beehive' can be seen as an imagery indicating the journey taken by learners in search for knowledge. But not all know how to tap into the beehives to procure the 'honey' that is knowledge in its most glorious form. Pedagogy becomes the skill set with which learners can have the means and methods to reach their goals. In other words, the choice of pedagogy is like a gateway to knowledge, having a large impact on how teaching and learning progress in a classroom.

The word 'pedagogy' comes from the Greek word '*paidagogos*' – in which '*paida*' means child and '*agog*' translates 'to lead the child'. Pedagogy can be defined as the science and art of education, specifically instructional theory. It can be seen as a master plan that includes a detailed analysis of what is to be done by a teacher.[12] The *Oxford Research Encyclopaedias* states that, 'Concepts of pedagogy that circulate within various educational contexts refer to the abstract and theoretical discourse about ways in which learners and students are introduced into fields of knowledge and established ways of knowing.'[13] The pedagogical aspect of education refers primarily to the ways in which learners and students are introduced into fields of knowledge and are inducted into learning about the established ways of knowing.[14]

The National Education Policy, 2020, emphasizes, among other things, the role of pedagogy in education.

> '…with the quickly changing employment landscape and global ecosystem, it is becoming increasingly critical that children not only learn, but more importantly learn how to learn. Education thus, must move towards less content, and more towards learning about how to think critically and solve problems, how to be creative and multidisciplinary, and how to innovate, adapt, and absorb new material in novel and changing fields. Pedagogy must evolve to make education more experiential, holistic, integrated, inquiry-driven, discovery-

> oriented, learner-centred, discussion-based, flexible, and, of course, enjoyable. The curriculum must include basic arts, crafts, humanities, games, sports and fitness, languages, literature, culture, and values, in addition to science and mathematics, to develop all aspects and capabilities of learners; and make education more well-rounded, useful, and fulfilling to the learner. Education must build character, enable learners to be ethical, rational, compassionate, and caring, while at the same time prepare them for gainful, fulfilling employment.[15]

Also important for our study is the concept of pedagogical analysis. The analysis of a given content in any subject, and any topic, needs to be carried out well in the spirit of the science of teaching (pedagogy). The methodology or process of instruction is vital. This focus on the teaching aspect is closely tied to the other half, the learning aspect.[16]

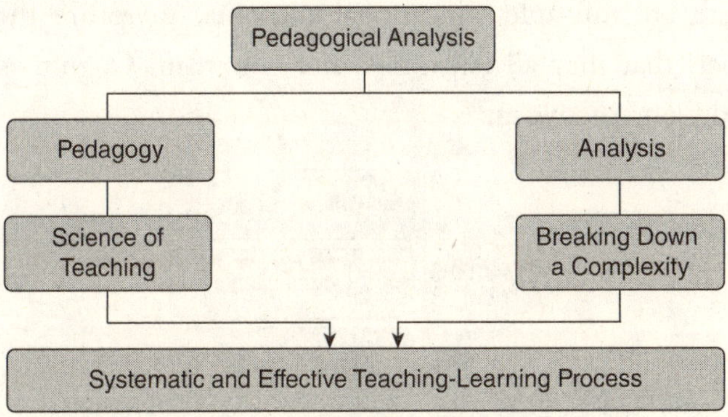

Fig 1: Pedagogical analysis[17]

Learning Theories

Since Plato, many theorists have emerged, all with their different takes on how students learn.[18]

Learning theories can be expressed as conceptual frameworks that explain how we best acquire, retain, recall and apply new knowledge and skills. These theories consist of premises and conclusions and are sometimes based on models or taxonomies. In other words, learning theories explain the processes that take place during learning and provide insights into the factors that influence us during this experience. Learning theories are considered to be remarkably useful tools for educators, instructors and trainers.

The choice of a learning theory often depends on the context, the nature of the subject matter and the preferences of learners. It is a good idea to have widespread knowledge of the options available to teachers.[19] Despite the fact that there are multiple educational theorists, there are three labels that they all fall under. Behaviourism, Cognitivism and Constructivism.[20]

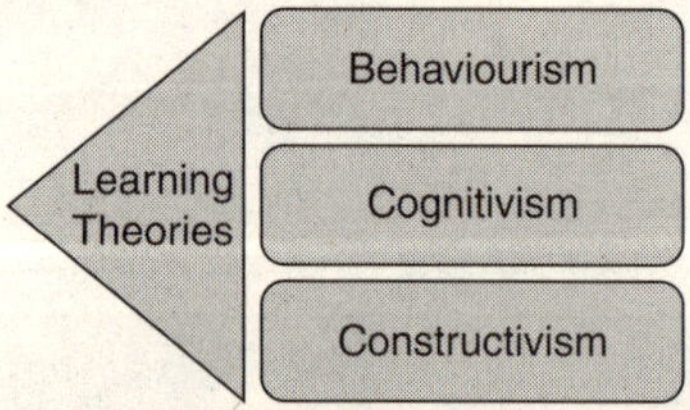

Fig 2: Classification of Learning Theories[21]

Behaviourism involves repeated actions, verbal reinforcement and incentives to take part. It is seen to be great for establishing rules, especially for behaviour management. This learning theory is based on the idea that knowledge is independent and on the exterior of the learner. For a behaviourist, the learner is a blank slate who should be provided with the information to be learnt. Through this interaction, new associations are made, and thus, learning takes place. Behaviourism emphasizes that learning is achieved when the provided stimulus changes behaviour.

In contrast to behaviourism, cognitivism focuses on the idea that students process information they receive rather than just responding to a stimulus. There is still a behaviour change evident, but this is in response to thinking and processing information. In cognitive load theory, scholars claim that learning occurs when the student reorganizes information, either by finding new explanations or adapting old ones.

Constructivism is based on the premise that we construct learning new ideas based on our own prior knowledge and experiences. Learning, therefore, to a constructivist is unique to the individual learner. Students adapt their models of understanding either by reflecting on prior theories or resolving misconceptions and need to have a prior base of knowledge for constructivist approaches to be effective. Bruner's spiral curriculum is a great example of constructivism in action.[22]

Behaviourism	Learning and behaviour changes are acquired by linking stimuli and response
Cognitivism	Learning is internal and is a result of a student processing and organising new information
Constructivism	Knowledge is constructed by adapting new information based on previous experience

Fig 3: Behaviourism, Cognitivism and Constructivism[23]

In the following pages, we will focus on this broad division and try to discuss how we can implement these theories in our classrooms.

Chapter 3

Behaviourism, Gamification

Behaviourism Learning Theory

Behaviourism is a theory that focuses on observable behaviours and external stimuli, without considering internal mental processes. In simple terms, this theory states that our behaviour is shaped by our environment, and as a result, one can teach new behaviours by conditioning learners' responses to stimuli. In the context of a learning programme, this means introducing positive and negative reinforcement for achieving the desired outcome. This theory emerged as a dominant force in psychology in the early twentieth century.[24]

QUICK FACT

B.F. Skinner, John B. Watson and Ivan Pavlov are considered the pioneers of modern behaviourism. According to a June 2002 survey, Skinner was listed as the most influential psychologist of the 20th century. He was also ranked by the American Psychological Association as the 20th century's most eminent psychologist.

Fig 4: B.F. Skinner,[25] John B. Watson[26] and Ivan Pavlov[27]

Positive reinforcement works by creating a feel-good association with the desired behaviour. When a child receives praise, a reward or even just a warm smile for their actions, their brain releases dopamine – the 'feel-good' neurotransmitter. This chemical surge creates a powerful motivation to repeat the behaviour in the future. It's like their brain is saying, 'Hey, that felt great! Let's do it again!'

But here's where it gets really interesting: The type of motivation matters. Extrinsic motivation, which comes from external rewards, can be a great starting point. However, the ultimate goal is to foster intrinsic motivation – the desire to engage in a behaviour for its own sake. It's like the difference between a child cleaning their room to earn screen time versus cleaning it because they enjoy the sense of accomplishment and the pleasant environment it creates.

As children grow and develop, their reward systems should evolve too. What works for a toddler might not cut it for a teenager. Age-appropriate reward systems consider a child's cognitive development, interests and increasing need for autonomy. It's a bit like adjusting the difficulty level in a video game – you want to keep it challenging enough to be engaging but not so hard that it becomes frustrating.

Now let's explore the buffet of reward systems available to us. There's no one-size-fits-all solution, so feel free to mix and match until you find what works best for you and your learners.[28]

Let's explore some easy-to-implement examples of positive reinforcement as teachers that we can use to support our learners:

1. **Badges:** In 1896, Benjamin S. Whitehead is known to have issued a patent for a button fastened to a metal pin, and thus, the badge as we know it today was born! The Boy Scout movement has been using badges to denote merit since as far back as 1909. Members can earn badges for demonstrating skills or achievements. These are sewn into their uniforms (or sashes, if you're in America) as a visual indicator of their progress.[29]
   Rewarding learners with badges acts as a form of positive reinforcement. This helps ignite a sense of achievement among young learners and motivates them to work diligently. Such badges can be part of a chart put up in classrooms and can be used to appreciate and encourage a number of activities, which can be as simple as good behaviour, observing school rules, discipline, completion of tasks, undertaking of community services, etc. The

idea behind this method is to see what the student is doing well, appreciate their strengths and encourage them to carry on with their praiseworthy actions.[30]

But what do we do if the student breaks school rules or does not complete her/his assignments frequently? For such instances, we have to be very cautious with our responses. A simple frowny can be put on the discipline board in classrooms to indicate to the child that certain acts of her/his is not being appreciated and should act as a reminder for the child to work on the matter. Teachers need to be mindful of the fact that a child should not permanently be assigned a frowny; any evidence of improvement should be noted and encouraged.

I remember in my school, after the end of each month, students were given certificates for good behaviour, code of conduct, discipline, etc., and now, after being a teacher, I realize that this effort by my class teachers to write such certificates every month was indeed a tedious task. But perhaps, I can now appreciate fully why they are so important. Even at this age, I have preserved all my certificates, academic and non-academic, as prized possessions. I can only imagine what effect it had on me as a student back then!

2. **Reminders:** Why do teachers want learners to write down their assignments in school diaries? This is because reminders can be powerful nudges, subtly encouraging learners to take action and stay on track.

A reminder board can be used in classrooms to allow students to glance at their tasks from time to time. For those schools using learning management platforms, a notification segment with reminders can directly influence behaviour.[31]

3. **Leaderboards, Experience Points:** Continuing with the idea of boards that will act as reminders of tasks for students, we can come up with leaderboards, which will provide a break-down of the top performers in each topic or lesson. However, this might pose a few challenges. A learner who does not see their name at the top of the board might feel demotivated to put in effort. So, this method works best if you have a small number of students, and that too a group that has similar learners and achievers.

   An even more nuanced and effective way of motivating students is the concept of Experience Points.[32] By this, learners are encouraged to reflect on their experiences and can also be made in charge of the experience points board, where they have the agency to give certain learning experience points and ask themselves what they learnt from the topic. This is a great way to recognize the most committed learners.

4. **Recognition:** How do we teachers feel when we are recognized for the hard work that we have put in all round the year? I am sure it definitely feels gratifying to some extent. Now think about the kids, who are

also looking for some kind of recognition from their teachers and peers. Recognizing their efforts, not just in academics but in all matters related to the child, can have wonderful effects on the level of motivation that she/he will have! Recognition does not always mean certificates; it can be expressed through a column in the school newsletter, a special mention during assembly or even a simple round of applause for the students for being such remarkable human beings!

Here, I cannot help but talk about a certain sequence from the movie *Stanley Ka Dabba*, directed by Amol Gupte. This 2011 film showcased the story of young Stanley (played by Partho Gupte), who studies in fourth grade in a school in Mumbai. Even when Stanley is a powerhouse of talent, not many teachers in his school could see through his mischievous demeanour and realize how brilliant the child is. Unlike his English teacher, Ms Rosy, played by Divya Dutta, most of his teachers do not think highly of Stanley. His science teacher, played by Divya Jagdale, rebukes his attempt at constructing a lighthouse as part of a class project since it does not adhere to the topics covered in class. She completely overlooks the imagination and high order thinking skills that are required by a child for such a project and which Stanley was able to effectively complete and present.[33] I am sure, like me, all of you had a similar disbelief as to how we adults often get so caught up in the monotony of schedules and the drudgery of daily life that we forget what imagination, creativity, effort and enthusiasm really look like!

Let's appreciate each child for her/his uniqueness.

5. **Feedback:** As teachers, we need to share positive and constructive feedback with our learners to motivate them to improve.[34] But what exactly do we mean by constructive feedback? Let us take a look at the following table to get a better idea: This can be delivered via quizzes, assessments, microunits and discussion forums (where relevant).

Not Constructive Feedback to Students	Is Constructive Feedback to Students
1. The student does not know how to write answers.	1. The student has some idea about the required answer structure. However, he/she needs to put in more effort to build up her/his writing skill. (Followed by what exactly the student needs to practise and improve – for example, arguments, evidencing, recall and expression of facts, analyses, etc.).

2. Student A is always late and never submits his homework.	2. Student A needs to reflect on his punctuality and behaviour when it comes to submitting his assignments. What is the importance of being on time? Why do we ask students to be particular about their submissions? Please get in touch with your teachers to share your reflections. After which, both of us will need to come up with a solution. We are in this journey together.

Can you come up with similar reframing of feedback based on your experience?

Not Constructive Feedback to Students	**Is Constructive Feedback to Students**
1.	1.
2.	2.

Criticisms of Behaviourism

As with any learning theory, there are a few things to be cautious of when integrating a behaviourism-backed approach into our teaching. Few psychologists today are strict adherents of behaviourism. Modern psychology considers it as one piece of a much larger puzzle of how we learn.

Behavioural learning theory can be seen to run the risk of oversimplifying things. For a start, it completely ignores our internal process, that is, our cognition. It neglects the role of thoughts, emotions and mental processes in shaping our actions. It also minimizes the impact of genetics, brain development and inherited predispositions on how readily we learn certain behaviours.

According to the Self-Determination Theory, autonomy is one of three psychological needs that motivate human action. If learners feel they don't have any control over their own lives, they're more likely to become disengaged. And in the light of these observations, we need to be cautious about what elements to take up and how we modify them to suit the needs of our learners. After all, Pavlov's experiment or Skinner's Box are examples of how the theory works, but human cognition is way too complex an element to be analysed just from the perspectives of conditioning and experiments.

Final Words

Behavioural learning theory offers a unique lens for understanding how our environment shapes us, and while a complete picture of human learning requires a broader approach, behavioural principles remain relevant – even to this day. The key here is to apply these principles ethically, always respecting learner agency and recognizing the influence of individual differences. Thankfully, there are a variety of methods that educators can use to achieve these ends. Let us not underestimate the power of feedback, reminders, recognition and a touch of healthy competition, etc. These have been shown to effectively ignite the much-needed spark among learners and ensure their engagement.[35]

Gamification as Pedagogy

Effective pedagogy recognizes the importance of informal learning. Studies have shown the significance of learning outside the formal context of the face-to-face or online course and indicates the value of using this in more formal educational contexts. The principle is about recognizing the enrichment value of everyday experience and implies that we need to build connections with the larger environment of learning.[36]

Why gamification? The *Oxford Online Dictionary* defines gamification as the application of typical elements of game playing (e.g., point scoring, competition with others and rules of play) to other areas of activity to encourage engagement. Gamification uses gaming principles in a non-game context. For example, learners can engage in activities to gather points and earn badges or scores. Thus, gamification taps into our inherent competitive spirit and desire to win. The resultant outcome is an increase in attentiveness and engagement, resulting in a higher level of learning and behaviour change.

Gamification stimulates the brain, causing the release of dopamine and endorphins. Dopamine is the hormone that generates good feelings when we complete specific actions. Endorphins are natural chemicals that reduce stress and anxiety. Achieving goals, receiving points and moving up a leaderboard trigger the release of these chemicals, compelling participants to return to engage with the content at hand.

Gamification's effectiveness is boosted by the fact that it creates a story around a topic. Stories help create an emotional connection with the content, thus making it easier to recall. Gamification goes one step beyond the recalling of information by inviting the learner to actively participate in the story, making it an even more memorable, immersive learning experience.[37]

Connecting the Dots: Behaviourism, Gamification and Activities

Mughal Maestros

Approximate duration: Flexible

Instructions and variations:

1. Students to participate individually or in groups.
2. To move on to the next round, students need to answer all the questions correctly.
3. The time allotted for each question to be decided by the teacher. The idea for this activity is to have a quick revision of a topic. The activity needs to be fast-paced.
4. A specific era of Mughal history can be allotted for each round. The following questions can be used as a guideline for teachers to make their own sets of questions.

Round 1: Babur

At what age did Babur become the ruler of Ferghana? (Answer: Twelve years)

In 1526, Babur's army clashed with the army of Ibrahim Lodi at ___________? (Answer: Panipat)

Who succeeded Babur as the Mughal emperor in India? (Answer: Humayun)

Round 2: Akbar

Students to encircle the places that witnessed military campaigns under Akbar on a map. Each correct answer will receive a point.

Round 3: Mughal architecture

(a) **Introduction to Agra Fort:** Agra Fort is one of India's most majestic historical monuments, filled with beautiful palaces, gardens, and audience halls built during the Mughal era. Imagine you're standing inside this grand fort, surrounded by history! Students will receive the architectural blue print of the fort and they will need to identify various segments of the fort. Then they create an exit route game on a blank blue print of the same fort.

(b) **Students' Task:** Let's go on a virtual adventure through the Agra Fort!

Yogesh has come to visit Agra Fort with his family. He enters through the Akbar Darwaza and wants to visit the following places:

- Moti Masjid
- Khas Mahal
- Anguri Bagh
- Diwan-i-Khas

Can you create a step-by-step guide or a set of clues to help Yogesh reach each of these places in the correct order?

For example:

1. From the Akbar Darwaza, Yogesh walks towards the white marble mosque that glows in the sunlight—this is the *Moti Masjid*!
2. Next, he turns toward the elegant palace built by Shah Jahan for his daughters, where he finds the *Khas Mahal*.
3. Surrounded by fragrant vines and beautiful symmetry, he now enters the *Anguri Bagh*.

4. Finally, he walks toward the place where the emperor met his special guests—the *Diwan-i-Khas*.

The National Education Policy 2020 states: 'A good education institution is one in which every student feels welcomed and cared for, where a safe and stimulating learning environment exists, where a wide range of learning experiences are offered, and where good physical infrastructure and appropriate resources conducive to learning are available to all students.' (Page 5, NEP 2020)

Games can help in achieving the aim of providing a stimulating, enriching learning environment for all students.

To make the activity even more interesting, teachers can use AI to design badges, which can be given to students with the highest score. The same can be transferred (or retained) by other learners in subsequent games conducted by the teacher for the subject. The following are examples of such designs created very easily using Meta AI:

Fig 5: Designs of badges for the highest scorers – Created by Meta AI

Social Learning Theory

This learning theory is often regarded as the bridge between behaviourism and cognitivism (discussed in detail in the following chapters). This is because it focuses on how mental (cognitive) factors are involved in learning. Its chief proponent, Prof. Albert Bandura, believed that humans are active information processors and they think about the relationship between their behaviour and its consequences. This theory emphasizes the importance of observing, modelling, and imitating the behaviours, attitudes and emotional reactions of others.[38]

But how exactly does imitation work? Let us look at a well-known story from our childhood to get an idea:

> Once in a small town, there lived a man who used to sell caps. The cap seller used to sell caps in all the nearby towns and villages. One day, as usual, he was starting his day. He decided to go to the next village to sell his caps in the village market.
>
> 'Caps, caps, caps! Five rupees caps, ten rupees caps!' said the cap seller loudly.
>
> Later, he was walking through the forest carrying a basket of colourful caps in his hands. He was tired of the sun's heat and thought of lying down under a tree for some time as he had walked a long distance. Putting his basket on the ground, he said to himself, 'I am so tired! Let me take a nap.'

There were many monkeys around him. Slowly, from one of the branches, a monkey peeped out. All of them were very naughty. One of them came down, and upon seeing the caps, he whistled. All the other monkeys responded to his whistle. One by one, they snatched away all the caps from the cap seller's basket. Everyone wore the caps and started playing happily.

When the cap seller woke up, he was shocked to see his basket empty. He searched for his caps everywhere. To his surprise, he saw the monkeys up in the tree wearing them. He tried various ways to get his caps back. He folded his hands and requested them to return the caps. The monkeys, in turn, simply mocked his actions by folding their own hands. He then raised his hands in anger, shouting at them to return the caps. The monkeys too raised their hands and started shouting. Finally, the cap seller used his common sense and realized that monkeys love to imitate. So, he used his smartness to get his caps back. He removed his own cap and threw it on the ground. Seeing this, the monkeys repeated the same. The cap seller quickly collected all the caps, placed them back in his basket and went back home happily.[39]

Not to say that children are like these naughty monkeys (though the classroom might feel like a jungle on some days!), but this humorous anecdote gives us an idea as to how imitation works.

Social learning theory can be defined as a theory of social behaviour. It proposes that new behaviours can be acquired by observing and imitating others. It states that learning is a cognitive process that takes place in a social context. This learning can occur purely through observation or direct instruction, even in the absence of direct reinforcement.[40] This is how the story of the cap seller and the monkeys can be used as an example to explain how learning takes place through observation or direct instruction.

The Social Learning Theory also states that in addition to the observation of behaviour, learning also occurs through the observation of rewards and punishments, a process known as vicarious reinforcement. When a particular behaviour is rewarded regularly, it will most likely persist. The opposite is also true – if a particular behaviour is constantly met with unrewarding outcomes, it will most likely desist. The theory expands on traditional behavioural theories in which behaviour is governed solely by reinforcements, by placing emphasis on the important roles of various internal processes in the learning journey of an individual.[41]

Albert Bandura shifted to a more cognitive perspective, and this led to a major revision of his social learning theory in 1977. At this time, the key tenets of the social learning theory were as follows:

1. Learning is not purely behavioural. It is a *cognitive* process that takes place in a social context.
2. Learning can occur by observing a behaviour *and* by observing the consequences of the behaviour (known as **vicarious reinforcement**).
3. Learning involves observation, extraction of information from those observations and making decisions about the performance of the behaviour. This is also known as observational learning or **modelling**.
4. For Bandura, reinforcement plays a role in learning but is not entirely responsible for learning.
5. The learner is not a passive recipient of information. Cognition, environment and behaviour all mutually influence each other, which is also called **reciprocal determinism.**[42]

Bandura created a famous series of experiments called the Bobo Doll experiments, which helped demonstrate his theory. In one of these experiments, Bandura created two groups of students: the control group and the test group. The control group of children watched an adult play calmly with a doll, and the test group watched an adult play aggressively with a doll. Afterwards, when the children got the chance to play with the dolls, the group who saw the adult play aggressively played more aggressively with the doll when it came to their turn, thus showcasing how we observe and learn.[43]

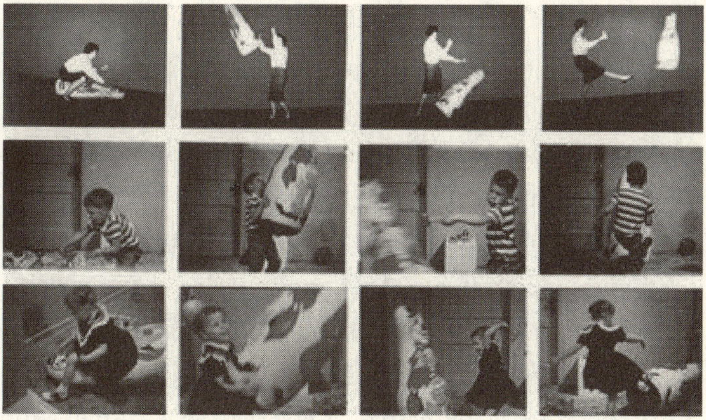

Fig 6: Bandura's Bobo Doll experiment[44]

Social learning theory will subsequently be merged with cognitive theories to develop the social cognitive theory.[45]

Experiential Learning as a Pedagogy

Experiential learning can be defined as a process of learning through experience. It is more narrowly defined as learning through reflection on doing. Hands-on learning can be a form of experiential learning but does not necessarily involve students reflecting on the resultant product. Experiential learning is distinct from rote learning, where the learner plays a comparatively passive role.

Experiential learning has important teaching advantages. Peter Senge, author of *The Fifth Discipline*, observes that teaching is of utmost importance to motivate people. Learning only has good effects when learners have the desire to absorb the knowledge, and therefore, experiential learning requires showing directions for learners.[46]

David Kolb described the ideal process of learning in a four-step Experiential Learning Cycle, which includes the following components:

Experiencing – Reflecting – Thinking – Acting.

1. **Experiencing (Concrete Experience):** Learning begins when a learner uses senses and perceptions to engage in what is happening now.
2. **Reflecting (Reflective Observation):** After the experience, a learner reflects on what happened and connects feelings with ideas about the experience.
3. **Thinking (Abstract Conceptualization):** The learner engages in thinking to reach conclusions and form theories, concepts or general principles that can be tested
4. **Acting (Active Experimentation):** The learner tests the theory and applies what was learned to get feedback and create the next experience.[47]

Pedagogy in Action

Promoting the Active Participation of Students in the Learning Process

Active participation is important in constructing knowledge and many opportunities should be provided for hands-on activities, project work, visits to nearby historical places, field work, interviews, report writing, using ICT for information retrieval, dramatics, etc.[48]

The National Curriculum Framework for School Education (2023) states that classroom processes should provide opportunities for students to work individually and to work together. Teachers may ensure that children work in pairs, small and large groups, as well as independently. Teachers should also help students to listen, understand, appreciate and reflect on their own thought processes and others' experiences with empathy and critical understanding.[49]

Effective pedagogy promotes the active engagement of the learner and is thus a key principle. 'This principle upholds "learners' independence and autonomy" and how this can be achieved to enhance learning. Becoming actively engaged supports learners to develop "positive learning dispositions".'[50]

Making classrooms inclusive is vital for student participation. The use of language that is inclusive of all learners could be the first step. Also, resources selected should reflect a diversity of perspectives and provide a variety of experiences.[51] All children should participate in a variety of activities and school processes, not just those with the best chances of success. Classrooms should have an environment that enhances the potential and interests of each child. Care is central to learning in schools and is an attitude of concern and responsibility for people and relationships.[52]

Interview and Documentary

An interview is a structured conversation where one participant asks questions and the other provides answers. The word 'interview' refers to a one-on-one conversation between an *interviewer* and an *interviewee*. The interviewer asks questions to which the interviewee responds, usually providing information and an answer to the question asked. That information may be used or provided to other audiences immediately or at a later time. An interview can also transfer information in both directions.

Interviews usually take place face to face or in person, but the parties may also be separated geographically, as in videoconferencing or telephone interviews. Interviews generally involve a spoken conversation between two or more parties but can also happen between two people who type their questions and answers.

Interviews can be in many forms. Unstructured, freewheeling and open-ended conversations are without a predetermined plan or prearranged questions. One form of an unstructured interview is a focused interview, where the interviewer consciously and consistently guides the conversation so that the interviewee's responses do not stray from the main research topic or idea. Structured interviews can also be highly organized conversations in which specific questions occur in a specified order. They can follow diverse formats; for example, in a ladder interview, a respondent's answers typically guide subsequent interviews, with the object being to explore a respondent's subconscious motives, which get reflected in the responses. Generally, the interviewer has some way of recording the information that is gleaned from the interviewee, often by keeping notes with a pencil and paper or with a video or audio recorder.

The traditional two-person interview format, sometimes called a one-on-one interview, permits direct questions and follow-ups, which enables an interviewer to better gauge the accuracy and relevance of collected responses. It is a flexible arrangement in that subsequent questions can be tailored to clarify earlier answers, and it also eliminates possible distortion due to other parties being present. Interviews can play an even more significant role, offering opportunities to showcase not just expertise but adaptability and strategic thinking.[53]

Panel Discussion

A panel discussion is a good way to engage students in meaningful and effective classroom discussions. A selected group of four to six students can act as panellists and the remaining students observe as the audience. The students in the panel conduct discussions around a particular topic but from different perspectives. One of the key benefits of the activity is that it provides an opportunity for learners to experience authentic, real-life, panel-based activities.

This activity also fosters productive learning relationships among students and allows them to reflect and think critically when listening to different viewpoints.

A few guidelines for organizing a panel discussion:

	Synchronous face to face	**Synchronous online**
Student Preparation	• Teachers to provide the relevant information and learning materials to students well before the panel discussion. • Discussion on the structure and assignment of roles needs to be done by the teachers. • Students to have an idea as to what is required of them. Teachers can provide detailed rubrics for the same. • Students need to be aware of the objective of the panel discussion. It should be a lively and robust discussion. • The students in the audience to prepare questions that they would like to ask the panellists.	• Teachers to provide the relevant information and learning materials to students well before the panel discussion. • Discussion on the structure and assignment of roles needs to be done by the teachers. • Students to have an idea as to what is required of them. Teachers can provide detailed rubrics for the same. • Students need to be aware of the objective of the panel discussion. It should be a lively and robust discussion. • The students in the audience to prepare questions that they would like to ask the panellists.

	Synchronous face to face	**Synchronous online**
Teacher Preparation	• Teachers to set up small groups of 3–4 students.	• Teachers to set up small groups of 3–4 students in breakout rooms.
During Activity	• Panellists (students) should take about 2 minutes each to present their viewpoint on the given topic. • After the panellists have spoken, the students taking part in the discussion can start asking questions and nominate the panellist to answer them. • The discussion to be closed at a pre-determined time.	• Panellists (students) should take about 2 minutes each to present their viewpoint on the given topic. • After the panellists have spoken, the students taking part in the discussion can start asking questions and nominate the panellist to answer them. • The discussion to be closed at a pre-determined time.
Artefact	• If the interaction has been filmed, this can be posted on a relevant site.	• If the interaction has been filmed, this can be posted on a relevant site.

To maximize participation, teachers may get the students to take turns to be panellists. Also, students can analyse a given topic under discussion and list the questions prior to the session. A moderator could be appointed from among the students. A follow-up activity can be considered that encourages students to reflect on the panel discussion and what they learned.[54]

Activity

Approximate duration: 40 minutes

Instructions and variations:

1. Students to choose any one leader associated with the Indian freedom struggle and research her/his ideas, methods, ideologies and the role played by the chosen leader in the struggle for freedom.
2. Students can then take part in a panel discussion and bring forth arguments based on the chosen leader.
3. Teachers can assign guiding questions for the panel to debate and discuss. For example: 'You have received the news of Chauri Chaura. What will your decision be on the progress of the Non-Cooperation Movement?' or 'What role should India play during World War II?', etc.

Activity

Approximate duration: Can vary on the basis of time available

Instructions and variations:

1. Students and teachers to set up interviews with the principal, vice principal or any other representative of the school.

2. A questionnaire could be mailed prior to the interview to the concerned person(s).
3. The project could be on the history of the institution and can be published online or in a print media resource after getting permission from the school.
4. The interview can help students to practise this particular method of learning on the school campus.

Chapter 4

Cognitivism, Social Learning Theory, Experiential Learning

Agatha Christie wrote 12 novels and 20 short stories featuring Miss Marple.[55]

The Guinness World Records awarded Sherlock Holmes the title for the 'most portrayed literary human character in film and TV' in 2012 and released a statement saying that the title 'reflects his enduring appeal and demonstrates that his detective talents are as compelling today as they were 125 years ago'.[56]

Satyajit Ray's Feluda, despite being a strongly built man adept in martial arts, relies mostly upon his superb analytical ability and observation skills, often humorously referred to as the *Magajastra* or brain weapon, to solve cases instead of using physical strength or weapons.[57]

The one thing that all these brilliant literary figures have in common is the intense use of cognition and cerebral effort to solve crimes.

Fig 7: Topshe and Feluda in Feludar Goendagiri, *written in 1965*[58]

Now, we might not be called upon to solve mysteries by using our cognitive abilities to learn. This is why teaching concepts based on cognitivism are of immense importance. Let us first understand what we mean by the term 'cognition'.

'Cognition' is 'the use of conscious mental processes'.[59] It is said to encompass all aspects of intellectual functions and processes such as perception, attention, thought, imagination, intelligence, the formation of knowledge, memory and working memory, judgement and evaluation, reasoning and computation, problem-solving and decision-making and comprehension and production of language. Cognitive processes are also known to use existing knowledge to discover new knowledge. [60]

Cognitivism is a theoretical framework to understand the mind. It gained increased currency in the 1950s. Many saw the movement as a response to behaviourism, which cognitivists said neglected to explain cognition. According to cognitivists, we have a complex physiological structure that absorbs a variety of stimuli from the environment, stimuli being the interactions that are able to produce knowledge and skills. Parents process such knowledge informally at home, while teachers process knowledge formally in school. This process of assimilating and expanding our intellectual horizon is termed cognitive development and is crucial for teaching-learning to take place.[61]

QUICK FACT

René Descartes[62]

One of the first philosophers who focused on cognition and how we think was René Descartes.

He was born in 1596. Descartes was a French philosopher, scientist and mathematician, widely considered as a seminal figure in the emergence of modern philosophy and science. One of his best known philosophical statement is '*cogito, ergo sum*', which is widely translated as 'I think, therefore I am' (French: *Je pense, donc je suis*), found in *Discourse on the Method* [1637, in French and Latin, 1644] and *Principles of Philosophy* [1644, in Latin, 1647 in French].[63])

Descartes's statement on cognition, 'I think, therefore I am', became a fundamental element of Western philosophy. While other knowledge could be a figment of imagination, deception or mistake, Descartes asserted that the very act of doubting one's own existence served, at minimum, as proof of the reality of one's own mind. For Descartes, there must be a thinking entity, in this case the self, for there to be a thought.[64] Cognition, the act of 'thinking', is thus pivotal to any and all recognition.

This focus on cognition is found in the Cognitive Learning Theory, which suggests that our cognitive processes have a role to play in determining knowledge and behaviour. Mental operations like analysing, organizing and storing are used to understand the world around us and are thus vital for learning. In other words, cognitive learning theory opines that learning is influenced by both **external** and **internal** factors.[65]

Cognitivism suggests that we are more than just a product of our environment. We are active agents. According to Jean Piaget, pioneering Swiss psychologist, understanding experiences is the way to learn. As learners understand how their thinking impacts their learning and behaviour, they are able to assert more control over it. While behaviourism suggests that learners have a passive conditioned role in learning, cognitivism states that learners actually play a more active role. Let's now break down the key principles of cognitive learning theory.

- **Information Processing:** Cognitivism views the mind as a processor of information. Our mind doesn't just collect data; it organizes and makes sense of it.[66] Similar to a computer, our brains take in information (as input), process it, store it and retrieve it when needed (as output).[67]
- **Memory:** Our ability to store and retrieve information depends on the functioning of our memory. In other words, without memory, cognitive functioning is simply not possible. The cognitive learning theory foregrounds the role of memory (short-term and long-term) in a learning process.
- **Critical Thinking:** In this approach, learners are not passive recipients of information. Instead, they are actively engaged and use their problem-solving and critical thinking skills throughout the process.
- **Metacognition:** The theory also states that learners have awareness and control over their thought processes. This leads to the ability to plan, monitor and evaluate our own learning progress.[68]

- **Motivation:** It's hard to make progress if we can't summon up the desire to learn. So, motivation is another internal factor that plays a crucial role in how much effort we put into learning and how well we ultimately perform.

This line of thought blossomed in the work of Jean Piaget. Through his systematic studies of cognitive development, Piaget laid the groundwork for both cognitive learning theory and constructivism as we know them today.

For Piaget, children (learners) aren't just empty vessels waiting to be filled with knowledge. They are active participants in their own learning. They use internal processes to build and shape their understanding. As he puts it, 'I find myself opposed to the view of knowledge as a passive copy of reality.'

This process continually evolves as they progress through the four stages of cognitive development, which is discussed in the subsequent segment. This model of learning was developed by Piaget in the 1920s and '30s. Indeed, Piaget was one of the first to identify that children think and learn differently from adults. Albert Einstein termed this discovery 'so simple, only a genius could have thought of it'. To fully understand and appreciate Piaget's theory, it's important to understand his view on how learning happens most effectively. He believed this involved achieving a balance between two central concepts: Assimilation and Accommodation.

- **Assimilation:** This is the process by which learners fit new information into existing mental frameworks. In other words, it's like filing something away in a familiar folder in our brain.

- **Accommodation:** This process takes place when learners encounter something so new that it doesn't fit within any existing framework. As a result, there is a need to adjust or create an entirely new 'folder' for this information.[69]

QUICK FACT

Jean William Fritz Piaget was born in 1896. He was a Swiss psychologist known for his work on child development. He placed immense importance on the education of children. As the director of the International Bureau of Education, he declared in 1934 that 'only education is capable of saving our societies from possible collapse, whether violent or gradual'. By the end of the 20th century, Piaget was second only to B.F. Skinner as the most-cited psychologist.[70]

Jean William Fritz Piaget[71]

The stages, according to Piaget, can be described as follows:

(a) The Sensorimotor Stage (0–2 Years Old)

According to Piaget, our brains do not hold any memories during the earliest stages of cognitive development. Consequently, we live solely in the present and take in information through assimilation.

During this time, we explore the world through our senses and develop basic motor skills. That's why it's called the sensorimotor stage. However, towards the end of this stage, this begins to shift. We achieve 'object permanence', meaning we become aware that objects exist, even if they have been hidden from view. Additionally, a range of other cognitive abilities begins to materialize. These include self-recognition, deferred imitation and representational play.[72]

Thus, little Bink from the movie/book *Baby's Day Out* could identify the zoo or the construction site from the objects and animals he saw on his 'day out'. Though meant to be a light-hearted adventure comedy, the film was one of the most watched motion pictures of the '90s, and hence the use of it as a reference here!

(b) The Preoperational Stage (2–7 Years Old)

The preoperational stage is a fascinating period when language emerges and symbolic thinking takes root. It is here that children learn to use words and pictures to represent objects. For the first time, children start accommodating new ideas and adjusting their understanding. In turn, this helps to fuel their imagination, which enables cognitive growth through 'dramatic' play (or make-believe). This kind of play is considered to be one of the first demonstrations of metacognition in children.[73] I remember a story of my uncle who, like many other young cricket fans, loved to play the role of a cricketer with newspapers rolled up to serve as the bat, crunched up to make the ball and fanned out to make leg guards. He would hit the moment a ball was thrown at him and start running while making sure his cap fell off his head – just the way a batsman often lost his cap while running between the wickets. No one corrected him since these make-believe plays are a way by which children learn.

At this stage, children are perhaps the most curious. Young children ask almost 300 questions a day. However, our thinking is still egocentric, and we find it difficult to see things from the perspective of others.

(c) The Concrete Operational Stage (7–11 Years Old)

Stage three is a game-changer. Here, children develop powerful reasoning skills and begin to think logically about the world around them. This is the result of a better balance between assimilation and accommodation. This new-found ability gradually chips away at their egocentrism, allowing them to consider and understand other people's points of view. That's progress!

Unlocking logic helps thoughts to become more structured and organized whilst still very concrete. As a result, abstract thinking (such as hypothetical scenarios and complex emotions) may still be difficult to grasp.

(d) The Formal Operational Stage (12–15 Years Old)

The final stage is when abstract thinking truly blossoms. Here, teenagers and young adults can accommodate information more readily, reason about hypothetical situations and even develop theories. This helps to pave the way for scientific thinking, allowing them to formulate hypotheses and systematically solve problems.

By the time this stage finalizes (around 14–15 years old), adolescents have shed their training wheels and can think critically and solve problems independently. Furnished with deductive reasoning skills, they can now unravel complex situations and strategies for the future.

In other words, they're now equipped with the cognitive tools they need to navigate an increasingly complex world.[74]

Just think of Harry, Ron and Hermione from the book *Harry Potter and the Prisoner of Azkaban.* These 14–15-year-olds could navigate complex plotlines, hatch a prison break to rescue Sirius Black and also end up giving the end-of-term exam in Hogwarts!

Students process information they receive rather than just responding to a stimulus.

Cognitive theories were developed in the early 1900s in Germany and Austria from Gestalt psychology by Wolfgang Kohler.[75] Gestalt psychology or gestaltism is a school of psychology and a theory of perception that emphasizes the processing of entire patterns and configurations, not merely individual components.[76] In other words, Gestalt can be roughly translated to the organization of something as a whole, that is viewed as more than the sum of its individual parts.[77]

Gestalt psychology is often associated with the saying, 'The whole is greater than the sum of its parts.' It emerged as a rejection of basic principles of Wilhelm Wundt's and Edward Titchener's elementalist and structuralist psychology.[78] Structuralists seek to consider the adult mind as the total sum of experience from birth to the present and analyse it in terms of the simplest definable components of experience. They then want to discover how these components fit together to form more complex experiences, as well as how they correlate to physical events. To do this, structuralists employ and add introspection: self-reports of sensations, views, feelings and emotions.[79]

An aspiring structuralist makes audio recordings of his thoughts and feelings while listening to classical music, being sure to use only single adjectives. Or say, to study taste sensations, a researcher provides samples of three types of chocolate and asks the research participants to take notes on the sensations they feel while consuming each type.[80]

For Gestalt psychologists, these individual adjectives, or the sensations after consumption of each type of chocolate, will all work together to form the 'experience' of the classical music piece or the act of having the chocolates.

Similarly, cognitivism focuses on the idea that students process information they receive rather than just responding to a stimulus[81] (the adjectives or individual sensations). It has given rise to many evidence-based education theories, including cognitive load theory, schema theory and dual coding theory, as well as being the basis for retrieval practice.[82]

Cognitive Load Theory (CLT), as proposed by John Sweller, focuses on the cognitive processes involved in learning and how the cognitive load imposed on learners affects their learning outcomes. Sweller proposed three types of cognitive load.[83] (Cognitive load refers to the amount of information the working memory can hold at any given time. Most learners can handle a cognitive load of between three and seven separate pieces of information).[84] The following are the three categories mentioned by Sweller:

- **Intrinsic Cognitive Load:** Can be defined as the inherent difficulty or complexity of the learning materials or tasks. The intrinsic load is determined by the complexity of the content and the learner's prior knowledge.[85]

  In other words, intrinsic cognitive load refers to the innate difficulty of the task. For example, recalling the chronology of important Mughal emperors would be low intrinsic load, whereas explaining the reasons for the emergence and decline of Mughal rule in India would be a higher level of intrinsic load. It is observed that teachers can match the intrinsic load of a topic to the experience of the learner but can't do much to reduce the complexity of the topic. Teachers, however, can reduce the extraneous load.[86]

- **Extraneous Cognitive Load:** It is the load imposed by the instructional design, such as irrelevant information or poorly designed instructional materials.[87] Extraneous cognitive load is where we, as teachers, have the most control. This type of cognitive load is concerned with the material and environment we subject the students to. Poorly constructed materials and busy classroom environments can lead to the split-attention effect and add to extraneous cognitive load. The job of a teacher is to reduce this with the way the lessons are presented.

  For example, the use of too many conflicting principles during a lesson can affect the attention span of learners, causing them to get distracted, resulting in ineffective knowledge transmission and absorption. It is detrimental to cognitive load. This issue can be solved by reducing the materials down to only contain the elements that are required. Irrelevant images, distracting sounds or animations or even fonts that are difficult to read should be omitted. A monotone voice and complicated vocabulary also add to the extraneous load. I bet you're wondering how you can reduce extraneous load, right? Don't worry, we'll get to that in a bit.[88]

- **Germane Cognitive Load:** This relates to the processing and integration of new information into existing mental schemas, which facilitates learning and long-term retention.[89] When learners are subjected to new information, their brain gives it a classification and stores it in our long-term memory. This classification is known as schemas. Schemas are like folders in our memory where we store similar information. We also have behavioural schemas that store behavioural patterns like all things to do with driving a car, making a sandwich or ice skating, etc. The more you use these schemas (practice), the easier the retrieval of the knowledge.[90]

Germane load is what we actually want to happen. It is the capacity of the working memory to link new ideas with information in long-term memory. It is the 'a-ha' light-bulb moment when a student finally gets the connection. The more prior knowledge a student has, the more effective the germane load stage will be. Germane load is where metacognitive strategies come into play. It is where learners are aware of their thinking processes and are able to adapt new information accordingly.

Teaching students the prerequisite skills prior to having them undertake a more complicated task will help them construct new schemas that strengthen their working memory and deal more effectively with germane cognitive load. This means that pre-training, or teaching people prerequisite skills before introducing a more complex topic, will help them establish schemas that extend their working memory. They can then understand and learn more difficult information effectively.[91]

According to the cognitive load theory, effective learning occurs when cognitive load is managed appropriately. High cognitive load can overwhelm learners' working memory capacity, thus leading to cognitive overload, which can impair learning. This theory suggests that learning tasks should be designed to minimize extraneous cognitive load and optimize germane cognitive load, allowing learners to focus their cognitive resources on understanding and integrating new information.[92] Let us take the help of some topics from social studies to understand how we can achieve the above goals by looking into some usable examples.

Agenda: Optimizing Germane Load

Learning tasks should promote active engagement and deep processing of information to optimize germane cognitive load. This may involve:

- Encouraging elaboration and reflection on new concepts.
- Providing opportunities for practise, feedback and reinforcement.
- Fostering metacognitive awareness and self-regulated learning strategies.[93]

Topic: Climate Change (Geography)

In the following activity, we will see how we can encourage elaboration and reflection on new concepts.

Fishbowl Discussion

In a fishbowl discussion, students inside the 'fishbowl' actively discuss a topic while those outside the fishbowl listen carefully to the conversation. Students take turns in these roles to practise being both contributors and listeners in a group discussion. A fishbowl activity is also useful to make sure all students participate in a discussion.[94]

Approximate duration: 40–50 minutes

1. Teachers can help in the selection of a topic for discussion. The most effective topics do not have one right answer or interpretation, but rather, allow for multiple perspectives and opinions. The fishbowl method is an excellent activity for discussing dilemmas, for instance.[95] 'Climate Change Policies' can be one such effective prompt, wherein the adequacy of current global initiatives to combat climate change can be discussed. Students advocating the cause can argue for more ambitious policies, emphasizing the urgent need to address environmental issues, while students who are more sceptical of the stance may question the feasibility, economic impact and effectiveness of proposed measures.[96]

2. Set up the room. A fishbowl conversation typically requires a circle of chairs and enough room around the ring for the remaining learners to observe what is happening in the fishbowl. Teachers can place enough chairs for half of the learners in the class to sit in the fishbowl, while at other times, the number can be further limited. Generally, six to twelve chairs allow for a range of perspectives while still allowing each learner to speak.
3. Prepare for the discussion and set up norms and rules for the activity. Like many formatted guided conversations, fishbowl discussions are most effective when learners have had several minutes to create ideas and questions beforehand. There are a lot of ways to format a fishbowl conversation. Teachers can have half the class sit in the fishbowl for 10 to 15 minutes before announcing 'Switch,' at which point the active listeners enter the fishbowl, and the speakers become the audience.

   Another format of fishbowl discussion is the 'tap' system, where learners on the outside of the fishbowl gently tap a learner on the inside, indicating that they must switch roles. Yet another way is to allow learners to look at a question or the content from various perspectives. Teachers can help assign perspectives to groups of learners. These perspectives could embody the viewpoints of different policies, historical figures, characters in a novel, social categories or philosophical points of view. Every group discusses the same question or content, embodying the assigned perspective. The goal of this technique is for learners to consider how perspective shapes meaning-making. After all the groups have shared, learners can be allowed to discuss their ideas and questions with peers from other groups. Regardless of which format is followed, it is essential that teachers establish the rules of the activity to the learners beforehand. Providing instructions for the learners in the audience, as well in the fishbowl, is very important. Before starting, teachers may also wish to review guidelines for having a respectful conversation. Sometimes, teachers ask the audience members to pay attention to how these norms are followed by recording specific aspects of the discussion process, such as the number of interruptions, examples of respectful or disrespectful language being used or speaking times.

4. After the discussion, teachers can ask learners to reflect on how they think the conversation went and what they learned from it. Learners can also assess their performance as active listeners and as performers. They could also give suggestions on how to improve the quality of discussion in the future.[97]

For our topic 'Climate Change Policies', the last phase of reflection is especially important as it will help give a possible guideline as to what steps we can take individually and as a community in relation to climate change. This will also help students to practise their critical thinking and problem-solving skills.

Topic: The Indian Constitution (Civics)

By the following activity, we will see how we can provide opportunities for practise, feedback and reinforcement.

Approximate duration: 40–50 minutes

Instructions:

1. This activity will draw on the prior knowledge of the students in relation to the topic at hand. Teachers can start a lesson with this activity or can introduce it after teaching the content.
2. If used as an activity to start the topic, teachers can ask students to think: What is a constitution? And how will we come up with a constitution for the class?

Students can be selected (or elected) in different committees decided by the teacher. Students also need to be guided as to the role and function of a particular committee (for example, discipline committee, cleanliness committee, class board committee, etc).

The students will then be allotted time to work in these committees to come up with their provisions, rules and regulations for the class.

Finally, there could be a common meeting for all the committees to decide on the draft constitution of the class, which then can be submitted to the teacher.

The following is an example of a class constitution drawn up by my own middle school students:

OUR CLASS CONSTITUTION!

WE, THE STUDENTS OF GRADE 6A TO REVIEW THE FOLLOWING RECOMMENDATIONS AND COME UP WITH A CONSTITUTION FOR OUR CLASS.

DISCIPLINE COMMITTEE'S RECOMMENDATIONS:

1. To have a peaceful class, we will raise our hands for answering a question.
2. We will follow the bell for staying on time.
3. Selection for class monitors to help maintain discipline.
4. switch off lights and fans before leaving the classroom.

CLEANLINESS COMMITTEE'S RECOMMENDATIONS:

1. Paper bins to be placed in every classrooms.
2. Dusters to be dusted outside the classroom.
3. After meal breaks, tables to be cleaned properly.

CLASS-BOARD COMMITTEE'S RECOMMENDATIONS:

1. All home-works to be written down at the side of class-boards by monitors.
2. With the help of teachers, charts to be put up regularly.
3. Birthdays to be written down too and put up on the boards.

If, however, the activity is used after the teacher has taught the content in class, the following modifications can be made to serve the agenda of optimizing the germane load by providing practise, feedback and reinforcement.

1. After learning the topic, the Indian Constitution, students will be able to identify how we came up with our

Constitution. Teachers can divide the class into groups and ask students to take the lead, thus implementing learner agency in the process

Students can be selected (or elected) in different committees based on the ones we had during the constitution-making process after Indian Independence. Students then need to research what the role and function of a particular committee was, along with other details significant for the working of the committee (for example – discipline committee, cleanliness committee, class board committee, etc).

The students will then be allotted time to work in these committees to understand and reflect how and why the constitution makers of India came up with their set of provisions, rules and regulations for the country.

Finally, there could be a presentation, where all committees come up to share their reflections of working in the different groups and also discuss, give feedback on the process of constitution-making and the main provisions of the Indian Constitution.

Topic: Decline of the Indus Valley Civilization (History)

By this activity, we will try to foster metacognitive awareness and self-regulated learning strategies.

Metacognition can be described as 'thinking about one's own thinking'. There are two aspects of metacognition: reflection – thinking about what we know and self-regulation – managing how we go about learning. Together, these processes make up an important aspect of learning and development. Metacognitive awareness means being aware of how we think. Metacognition, then, can be explained as the awareness of one's thinking and the strategies one is using. It enables learners to be more mindful of what they are doing, and why and how the skills they are learning might be used differently in different situations.[98]

Think-Pair-Share

Approximate duration: 30–40 minutes

1. Teachers to assign a question or present a problem to students and give them around 1–5 minutes to think through (or write down) their response.
2. Next, students to turn to a partner and discuss their ideas on the given question or problem.
3. Finally, students to share what came up in their pair discussions during a whole class discussion. For our topic, 'Decline of the Indus Valley Civilization', students can refer to the multiple theories: natural disasters, change in the course of the Indus River, Aryan invasion theory, gradual decline theory, etc.[99]

Agenda: Minimizing Extraneous Load

Instructional materials should be carefully designed to minimize extraneous cognitive load. This may involve:

- Simplifying instructions and explanations
- Using clear and concise language

- Presenting information in a structured and organized manner
- Minimizing distractions and irrelevant information[100]

Example: Look at the following two explanations on the solar system. Mark which explanation you think will be more useful in class while teaching the topic to your students:

Explanation 1: The solar system is a group of objects that are all held together by the sun's gravity. These objects include:

1. **The Sun:** This is a giant ball of hot gas at the centre of the solar system. It provides light and heat, which makes life on earth possible.
2. **The Planets:** There are eight planets that orbit the sun. They are:

   Mercury, **Venus**, **Earth** (our planet), **Mars**, **Jupiter**, **Saturn**, **Uranus** and **Neptune.**

   These planets are of different sizes, and some have moons that orbit around them, like earth has the moon.
3. **Dwarf Planets:** These are smaller than regular planets, for example, Pluto.
4. **Moons:** Many planets have moons, which are like small natural satellites that orbit around them. Earth's moon is an example.
5. **Asteroids and Comets:** There are small, rocky objects called asteroids and icy objects called comets that travel through space.[101]

Explanation 2: The solar system, a rather intricate expanse, is essentially an astronomical aggregation of celestial bodies that revolve around a central, immense luminous sphere of plasma, also known to human beings as the sun. This heliocentric collection comprises a variety of planetary bodies, each possessing unique orbital characteristics. These planets, from the inner rocky entities to the gaseous giants in the outer realms, are intricately bound to the sun through gravitational forces, which manifest in elliptical orbits of varying eccentricities. The planetary bodies themselves are accompanied by numerous satellites, often referred to as moons, which exhibit a diverse array of orbital periods and compositions. A considerable number of these moons are tethered to their respective planetary hosts with an almost mesmerizing consistency. Beyond the planetary ensemble lies a swath of diminutive objects such as asteroids and comets, which occupy the less densely populated regions of the solar system, their erratic trajectories often punctuated by brief interludes of near-perihelion passage. In sum, the solar system is an enigmatic collection, a gravitationally unified but otherwise complex web of interactions, whose celestial components oscillate in perpetuity, bound by forces that continue to challenge full comprehension.[102]

Agenda: Managing Intrinsic Load

'Teachers should scaffold learning by breaking down complex concepts into smaller, more manageable chunks. This may involve:

- Providing worked examples or step-by-step demonstrations.

- Gradually increasing the complexity of tasks as learners gain proficiency.'[103]
- Topic: Why did the Renaissance start in Italy?
- By using this activity, we aim to provide worked examples or step-by-step demonstrations.

Scaffolding

Scaffolding can be considered as a form of both demonstration and discussion, which can be used by learners to understand a given topic.

A scaffold is a temporary support that is used to assist a learner and is gradually withdrawn as learners become more competent. Scaffolds can include modelling the steps by the teacher or thinking aloud by the teacher as she or he solves the problem. It can be tools, such as cue cards or checklists, that complete part of the task for the students or a model of the completed task against which students can compare their own work. Such a process of helping students solve difficult problems by modelling and providing scaffolds has been called 'cognitive apprenticeship'. Students learn strategies and content during this apprenticeship that enable them to become competent readers, writers and problem-solvers.

One form of scaffolding is to give students prompts for steps they might use. Prompts such as 'who', 'why' and 'how' have helped students learn to ask questions while they read. Teachers might think aloud while solving a scientific equation or writing an essay, and at the same time, provide labels for their mental processes, thus providing learners with a way to observe 'expert thinking' that is usually hidden from the student. Studies have shown the usefulness of giving students a checklist to evaluate their work. Checklist items included guiding questions like 'Have I found the most important information that tells me more about the main idea?' and 'Does every sentence start with a capital letter?' The teacher then modelled the use of the checklist. In other situations, students were provided with expert models with which they could compare their work. For example, when students were taught to generate questions, they could compare their questions with those generated by the teacher.[104]

Students can easily learn new knowledge when systematic support from other experienced students or teachers is provided. Learning new knowledge can be a challenge, but the challenge should be within the reach of students – something that relates to their existing knowledge and can be done with the support of an experienced person. The 'Gradual Release of Responsibility' (GRR) is where, first, teachers model or explain ideas or skills, after which students and teachers work together on the same ideas and skills, where the teacher provides guided support, and finally, students practise individually and independently.[105]

Worksheet using the technique of scaffolding:

Name: Grade:

Date: Subject: History

Instructions to students: Using the guiding questions, complete the answer to 'Why did the Renaissance start in Italy?'

1. This is a causation question. So think of one reason that led to the Renaissance as a movement in Italy.

   ____

   ____

   ____

   ____

   (Keywords for this point could be wealth, patronage, Medici, Florence, art)

2. Very good! Now, think of another cause for the Renaissance to take place in Italy. Remember, you are answering a WHY question.

   ____

   ____

   ____

   ____

   (Keywords for this point could be location, trade, exchange of ideas)

3. Well done! Now, let's think about one more point, shall we?

   ____

   ____

   ____

   ____

   (Keep on questioning yourself with the word WHY. Keywords here could be the ancient Roman Empire, rediscovery of the past, Greek and Roman texts.)

A note for the teachers will be to mention the marks that each correct point and effective explanations will carry. This will further help students in planning the answer and then expressing themselves accordingly.

Topic: To have true democracy is to have zero poverty. (Civics)

This activity will help in a gradual increase of the complexity of tasks as learners gain proficiency.

Socratic Circle

The Socratic Circle approach is a structured, dialogue-oriented and student-driven discussion that takes place with the teacher as a guide and facilitator rather than as a 'sage on the stage' or a 'guide on the side'. It involves a structured discussion where students arrange themselves in two concentric circles, forming two distinct groups. Members of the 'inner circle' are actively involved in discussion with one another while the students in the 'outer circle' take notes, observe and notice patterns within this discussion. As discussants, students are provided with a prompt or initiating questions, mainly by the teacher. The questions can be closely tied to a written article they have read and annotated closely prior to the discussion.[106]

Some key benefits of the Socratic Method/Socratic Circle could be summarized as follows:

- Enhanced critical thinking skills
- Improved problem-solving abilities
- A deeper understanding of a given topic

- Development of communication and observational skills
- Promotion of higher-order thinking and metacognition[107]

Activity

Approximate duration: 30–40 minutes

Instructions and variations:

1. Students to form two circles – an inner circle and outer circle. The diagram attached herewith can also be used as a reference while forming these circles.
2. As the students of the inner circle discuss, the outer circle observes. Then, the outer circle comes up with questions and observations based on their study of the discussion of the inner circle.
3. Additionally, the circles can change places and repeat the activity or take up other factors of the chosen topics. Teachers can help in increasing the complexity of the topic by adding information that needs further and intense brainstorming.
4. Teachers to assign sub-topics and guide the discussion at all levels.

We sometimes encounter the question: What is the link between instruction and cognitive processes? If study materials are already available to students, what then is the role of a teacher? Why is it extremely important for teachers to design and implement their teaching effectively if learners already possess the learning materials – textbooks, online resources, etc?

Robert Gagné 's Nine Events of Instruction

To answer all the above questions, we must take help from Robert Gagné's Nine Events of Instruction. Gagne's pedagogical strategies for teaching focuses on teacher-centred classrooms. In these classrooms, there is an outline of a structured sequence of actions for the instructor to follow to effectively deliver instruction. The events in the sequence highlight the teacher's role in planning, organizing and facilitating learning experiences for students. Each event is designed to guide the teacher in engaging students, presenting content, providing guidance and assessing learning for effective teaching-learning to take place.[108]

QUICK FACT

Born in 1916, Robert Mills Gagné was an American educational psychologist who is best known for his *Conditions of Learning* (Published in 1965, describing Gagné's eight kinds of learning and nine events of instruction). He is known to have instructed during World War II, when he worked with the Army Air Corps training pilots. He went on to develop a series of studies and works that simplified and explained what he and others believed to be good instruction. His work is sometimes summarized as the *Gagné assumption*, which states that different types of learning exist, and that different instructional conditions are most likely to bring about these different types of learning.

Robert Gagné's work is considered to be the foundation of instructional design since the beginning of the 1960s, when he researched and developed training materials for the military. Among the first to coin the term 'instructional design', Gagné developed some of the earliest instructional design models and ideas, which continues to inspire educationists, teachers and researchers even today.

Prior to Robert Gagné, learning was often considered as a single, uniform process, with little or no distinction made between 'learning to load a rifle and learning to solve a complex mathematical problem'. Gagné offered an alternative view, which developed the idea that different learners required different learning strategies and understanding, designing instruction based on a learning style defined by the individual that brought about new theories and approaches to teaching. His understanding and theories of human learning added significantly to understanding the stages in cognitive processing and instructions.[109]

Nine Events of Instruction

According to Gagné, learning occurs in a series of nine learning events. Each of these learning events is a condition for learning that must be accomplished before moving to the next in order. The instructional events (executed by the instructor/teacher) should mirror the learning events:[110]

1. **Attract Attention:** This involves captivating learners' interest through relevant stimuli. Thought-provoking

questions can also be used to gain the attention of the learners before they start to process any new information.

2. **State Objectives:** Teachers to clearly communicate the learning goals to focus learners' attention and motivate them. By being aware of the learning objectives, the students will be better able to focus on the requirements of the content.
3. **Activate Prior Knowledge:** Engage learners by connecting new information to what they already know. This link with the existing knowledge will help in the absorption of new knowledge.
4. **Deliver Content:** Presentation of the instructional material in a logical sequence is very important. Teachers can use various strategies, such as lectures or multimedia, to deliver the content.
5. **Provide Guidance:** Teachers to support learners by offering explanations, examples and instructions to aid understanding. By providing organization and relevance, teachers to make the content more 'memorable' for students.
6. **Encourage Practise:** Teachers to offer opportunities for learners to apply newly acquired knowledge or skills actively. This demonstration of what has been learned is useful for the teacher to comprehend the level of learning that has taken place.
7. **Offer Feedback:** Providing feedback on the performance of the learners and reinforcing correct understanding

should be the next step. This will help learners identify the areas for improvement.

8. **Evaluate Performance:** To reinforce learning, assessment of the learners' progress using multiple methods like quizzes, tests or practical exercises will help the teacher to gauge the achievement of the pre-stated learning objectives.
9. **Facilitate Retention and Transfer:** Teachers to employ strategies like review and application in different contexts to promote long-term retention and application of learned material.[111]

Let us take a look at the following examples to see how we can use Gagné's Nine Events of Instruction for teaching social studies in our classrooms:

Event	**Examples**	**Cognitive Process**
Attract Attention	Good morning students! Tell me, how many of you are truly following the Lok Sabha elections news every day?	Reception
Identify Objective	Today, we will learn about how we elect our government. (Teachers can write on the board: WALT – what are we learning today – followed by the topic for the lesson.)	Expectancy
Recall Prior Learning	Last lesson we learned about Democracy – what do we remember?	Retrieval

Event	Examples	Cognitive Process
Present Stimulus	Here are the broad categories of government we have in our country – Central, State.	Selective Perception
Guide Learning	Here are some examples of parties that have formed governments in the past	Semantic Encoding
Elicit Performance	List the process of elections that you think needs to take place.	Responding
Provide Feedback	You are thinking along the correct lines! Let's take a look at what our textbook says.	Reinforcement
Assess Performance	All of you have given thought-out responses to the end of chapter questions on what we have learned today. Very good, students!	Retrieval
Enhance Retention/ Transfer	Now copy down the following questions and determine whether the statements are true or false in relation to how we elect our government.	Generalization

Fig 8: Table based on Gagné's Nine Events of Instruction[112]

Now, it is your turn, dear readers, to come up with your own examples for a subject/topic of your choice and fill in the table below. Practise indeed makes a huge difference!

Event	Examples	Cognitive Process
Attract Attention		Reception
Identify Objective		Expectancy
Recall Prior Learning		Retrieval
Present Stimulus		Selective Perception
Guide Learning		Semantic Encoding
Elicit Performance		Responding
Provide Feedback		Reinforcement
Assess Performance		Retrieval
Enhance Retention/ Transfer		Generalization

In order to evaluate instruction, teachers can introspect and ask themselves questions like: Have the objectives been met? What is the general absorption level of the content taught today among my students? What additional effects do I need to include in my instruction to make it more effective? Some educators believe that Gagné's taxonomy of learning outcomes and events of instruction have a tendency to oversimplify the learning process by over-prescribing. However, using them as part of a complete instructional package can definitely help many educators in becoming more organized and staying focused on the instructional goals. In his 'The Idea of Schema', Gagné wrote, 'Since the purpose of instruction is learning, the central focus for rational derivation of instructional techniques is the human learner. Development of rationally sound instructional procedures must take into account learner characteristics such as initiate capacities, experimental maturity, and current knowledge states. Such factors become parameters of the design of any particular program of instruction.'[113]

Ausubel's Reception Learning Theory

In 'Ausubel's Learning Theory: An Approach to Teaching Higher Order Thinking Skills', we find a detailed analysis of how Ausubel's Learning Theory can be linked and implemented to teach learners the skill of higher-order thinking and other cognitive processes. For Ausubel, thinking is an orderly activity and knowledge is arranged in a hierarchical pattern. In this hierarchy, the higher-level concepts subsume lower-level ones. According to Ausubel's theory, learning is largely a matter of fitting new information into an already existing cognitive structure, and retention and forgetting are two different aspects of the same psychological process, subsumption, all of which fit together in a logically consistent system.[114]

In other words, Ausubel's Reception Learning Theory (also known as Meaningful Reception Theory) emphasizes the importance of meaningful learning by actively integrating new information into existing cognitive structures.[115]

QUICK FACT

David Paul Ausubel came to educational psychology from the field of medicine.[116] His development and research on 'advance organizers' is considered to be his most significant contribution to the fields of educational psychology, cognitive science and science education learning. Ausubel believed that an understanding of concepts, principles and ideas is achieved through deductive reasoning.[117] Deductive reasoning can be explained as the process of drawing valid inferences.[118]

Ausubel's reception learning involves the following:

Advance Organizers: Ausubel introduced the concept of advance organizers, which can be described as introductory materials or activities designed to provide a framework for understanding new information. These organizers help learners connect new concepts with their existing knowledge and mental frameworks, thus facilitating meaningful learning.

Example: Mind maps

Mind map, developed by Tony Buzan as a note-taking technique, is an application that has the power to uncover the thoughts in the brain about a subject from different viewpoints. This technique also helps in activating the right and left lobes of the brain together as an alternative to linear thought. It is observed that mind maps have benefits such as recalling, improving creativity, solving problems, focusing on a subject and organizing the thoughts of learners. Mind maps have an important place as a lifelong learning tool and are vital for the learning-teaching process.

Tony Buzan emphasizes four important features of mind maps as:

- Attention to the subject could be provided by a picture at the centre of the mind map.
- Main themes, criteria of the subject are created in the form of the branches related to the picture at the centre.
- The branches state a key picture or keyword using the connected lines.
- The branches have a structure that is related to the other branches.[119]

T. Steyn and A. Boer, in their studies, concluded that learners enjoy using the mind map technique and remember easily what they learned with the help of this technique.

K. Goodnough and R. Woods are of the opinion that students express positive opinions about mind mapping, and find this technique interesting and enjoyable.[120]

Activity

Topic: The Revolt of 1857

Approximate duration: 30 minutes

Instructions and variations:

1. Teachers to assign a segment of the given topic, like 'Reasons for the Revolt of 1857' or 'Results of the

Revolt'. Students can use the blank mind map provided below as a reference for the activity.

2. Alternatively, mind maps can be created digitally as well using various websites.

Subsumption: In his theory, Ausubel proposed the idea of subsumption, which involves incorporating new information into existing cognitive structures or 'subsumers'. When learners encounter new information that is relevant and meaningful, they tend to assimilate it into their existing knowledge base, thereby enhancing understanding and retention.

Example: People scavenge

This is a fun activity to do at the start of the school year. Here, we take the idea of Thomas N. Turner and ask the students to interview their peers about what they know and have experienced. They must not have data for more than three items from the same individual. Teachers can then record the results, such as how long it took and how many questions could be answered. Then, at the end of the school year (during which the teacher has emphasized current events in the classroom), the same activity can be repeated, and the results can be compared. Teachers can then estimate whether the students' 'news knowledge' improved as a result of the emphasis on current events.

The following can be used as a framework for questions asked during this activity. Also record the initials of students who have successfully done the point mentioned:

- Can you name two TV anchors?
- Can you name three countries that were in the news last week?
- Do you know something about a natural disaster that was in the news in the last two years?
- Can you name at least three different sections of the newspaper?
- Can you name at least two different jobs in a newspaper?
- Can you name two national news magazines?
- Have you listened to the news on the radio or watched a bulletin on TV in the last day?
- Can you name three cities that were in the national news last week?
- Can you name the leaders of three countries other than the country you live in?
- Can you name the president and the prime minister?

Meaningful Learning: Ausubel emphasized the importance of meaningful learning, by which learners actively relate new information to their existing knowledge and experiences. Rather than rote memorization or passive reception of facts, meaningful learning involves making connections, organizing information and creating meaningful associations.

Example: Model making

Model making can be done in small groups to instil collaboration skills among young learners. Students will also get an opportunity to think critically and get a primary idea of the different nuances of building an architectural monument. This will not only help in a better understanding of the topic at hand but also encourage students to bring out their creativity.

Activity

Topic: How did the inhabitants of Mohenjo-Daro solve the problem of drainage and water leaking in the Great Bath? Approximate duration: Assembling time using pre-made parts: 40 minutes

Instructions and variations:

1. Students to choose any prominent feature of the Indus Valley civilization (for example: the Great Bath at Mohenjo-Daro or the structure of the citadel and surrounding lower town, etc.) and make a model representing the chosen site.
2. The emphasis will be on studying the selected site in detail and replicating it as realistically as possible in the model.
3. The model can be made using readily available materials like clay, plasticine, etc.

Hierarchy of Learning: According to Ausubel, learning occurs in a hierarchical fashion, with new knowledge being integrated into existing cognitive structures in a structured and organized manner. Learners are considered to build upon their prior knowledge and understanding, progressively expanding and refining their conceptual frameworks.

Example: Book review

A book review is a critical evaluation of a book, offering insights into its content, quality and impact of the work and helps readers make informed decisions about whether to read the book.[121]

For our context, we can use this learning strategy to go through the available sources of literary works that are connected to our subject and topic. They can be both fictional and non-fictional; however, the latter will be a more valuable source of information.

Writing a book review as an assignment benefits students in multiple ways, and the following are a few of them:

First, it teaches students how to write a book review by developing their analytical skills as they evaluate the content, themes and writing style.

Second, it enhances the learner's ability to express opinions and provide constructive criticism. Book review assignments also expose students to various publications and genres, broadening their knowledge.

Furthermore, these tasks foster essential skills for academic success, like critical thinking and the ability to synthesize information. [122]

The following template can be used to write a book review:

Introduction

- Discussion about the book cover and its title
- Mention of any subtitle
- Mention of the author's name

Thesis

- A brief description of the novel
- Introduction of the main points that will be discussed in the body
- Students to refrain from sharing opinions at this stage

Body

- Mention of 2–3 quotations from the book
- Summarization of each quotation in the student's own words
- Discussion of the student's viewpoint on each quotation
- Each point to be organized in separate paragraphs

Conclusion

- Summarization of each quotation and its explanation
- Crafting of a concluding sentence
- Sharing of final opinion on the book
- (Optional) Provision of a star rating[123]

Activity

Topic: The Indian Freedom Struggle

Approximate duration: 10–15 minutes per student/group

Instructions and variations:

1. Teachers to assign selected literary works on the Indian freedom struggle (for example, *Hind Swaraj* by Mahatma Gandhi, *The Discovery of India* by Jawaharlal Nehru, etc.) as homework and ask students to go through the

reading list and come up with a review.

2. The review can be in the form of a written work or a presentation.

Excerpt of a Book Review:

M.K. Gandhi's Hind Swaraj is a monumental work in the philosophy of civilization. It offers a powerful critique of modern civilization. Gandhi provides a sharp and incisive analysis of contemporary life, yet, regrettably, this brief text has not received the attention it deserves from philosophers. Gandhi was not only a prominent political leader but also a profound thinker and a critic of modern civilization. His observations may initially appear dogmatic, unusual, or even extreme; however, through this critique, he lays the foundation for a new social order.

Gandhi can be regarded as a social philosopher. Like many classical thinkers, he presents a distinct vision of the human being and of society. Hind Swaraj *may rightly be seen as the foundational text or "Bible" of Gandhian thought. This small book contains the earliest formulation of his core ideas. Even two or three decades after its publication, Gandhi saw no need to make significant changes to the text, aside from a few minor edits. He stated that he had consistently tried to live by the principles articulated in this work.*

The primary aim of the book is to critique Western civilization. In doing so, Gandhi attempts to outline the principles of a new way of life that would make both individual and social existence more meaningful. His views on politics, religion, and morality are embedded within this work. Originally written in Gujarati in 1908, Hind Swaraj *was later translated into English. Though modest in length, it stands as a masterwork of Gandhian philosophy. Many of Gandhi's later ideas can be traced back to this text in their embryonic form.*

Modern philosophy, especially as it has developed in the Anglo-American tradition, often emphasizes logical analysis, abstract concepts, and linguistic critique. This approach is largely rooted in the work of logical positivists, who argued that philosophy cannot provide direct knowledge of reality. According to them, philosophy's role is not to reveal truths about the world, but to clarify language and eliminate confusion. Gandhi's work, by contrast, challenges this narrow conception of philosophy and proposes a more holistic, value-driven approach to understanding human life and society.

Relevance and Significance: In his theory, Ausubel stressed the importance of presenting information in a way that is relevant and meaningful to learners. When new information is connected to learners' existing knowledge and experiences, it becomes more meaningful and easier to understand and remember.[124]

Example: Dynasty tree

A family tree is a chart representing family relationships in a conventional tree structure.[125]

A tree structure or tree model is a way of representing the hierarchical nature of a structure in a graphical form. It is named a 'tree structure' because the classic representation resembles a tree, even when the chart is generally upside down compared to a biological tree, with the 'stem' at the top and the 'leaves' at the bottom. The gender-neutral names 'parent' and 'child' have largely displaced the older terminology like 'father' and 'son'.[126]

The family tree can be applied to historical context, and we can come up with dynasty trees for studying the different phases of the Delhi Sultanate's history. This will enable visual representation of information, which will, in turn, help in better fact retention among students.

Activity

Topic: The Delhi Sultanate

Approximate duration: 30 minutes

Instructions and variations:

Teachers can create a family tree of one of the dynasties of the Delhi Sultanate to use as reference for this activity.

Recollection of chronological historical data might seem daunting to students. However, representing the various dynasties or monarchs in the form of a dynasty/family tree will help in both visualizing the order and also lead to better recollection of facts and figures.

Ausubel explained the concepts of retention and forgetting. First, information is believed to be more effectively retained by a learner when it is fitted into a system of mutually supporting ideas. Learners who have well-organized cognitive systems tend to retain information efficiently. On the other hand, learners who have displayed poorly organized cognitive systems tend to forget information rapidly. Asubel observed, 'It is largely by strengthening relevant aspects of cognitive structure that new learning and retention can be facilitated.'

Second, in order to explain why forgetting occurs, Asubel states that the more completely information is absorbed into its anchoring concept, the more it tends to lose its own distinctive character. Thus, when information is 'reduced to the least common denominator capable of representing it, namely, to the anchoring idea itself', it is said to be forgotten.[127]

Chapter 5

Cognitivism Continued: Cognitive Load Theory

Let us kick-start our understanding of the Theory of Multiple Intelligences by looking at the following two world-renowned personalities. Both can be considered as maestros in their respective fields.

Personality 1: Ustad Zakir Hussain, the eldest son of the legendary tabla maestro Ustad Alla Rakha, was immersed in the rich traditions of Indian classical music from an early age. Hussain had shared that his father welcomed him into the world by whispering the rhythms of the percussion instrument into his ears. And throughout his life, Hussain demonstrated his extraordinary talent for the instrument, receiving nominations for seven Grammy awards and winning four times India's highest honour for performing artists – the Padma Shri in 1988, the Sangeet Natak Akademi Award in 1990, the Padma Bhushan in 2002 and the Padma Vibhushan in 2023.[128]

Fig 9: Ustad Zakir Hussain[129]

The following QR code will take the teacher to a video of the *Teental-Peshkar* played by Ustad Ahmedjan Thirakwa.

What kind of skill set or category of cognition do you think a person needs to inculcate to master such musical intelligence?

Personality 2: Serena Williams, one of the greatest tennis players of all time, was ranked as the world No. 1 in women's singles by the Women's Tennis Association (WTA) for 319 weeks (third-most of all time) and finished as the year-end No. 1 five times. She is the only player to date to accomplish a career Golden Slam in both singles and doubles! Many players, commentators and sports writers worldwide regard Williams as the greatest female tennis player of all time.[130]

The following are some suggestions made by experts to tennis players to help them give their best.

'*Your Forehand is Your Best Shot. Your Opponent's Backhand is their Weakness. There are Three Ways to Win a Point. Recognize the Importance of the Serve. Don't Be Afraid to Lose the Point. Baseline Mastery…*'[131]

What kind of cognitive processes, skill sets do you think are associated with sports? Is it just about movement, or are there intense intellectual preparations that go behind each move that athletes spend years to master?

The depiction of intelligence modalities presented at the very beginning of the chapter will help us to understand and answer the above questions. The given diagram relates to the **theory of multiple intelligences**, which states that human intelligence is not a single general ability but comprises various distinct modalities, such as linguistic, logical-mathematical, musical and spatial intelligences. The concept was introduced by Howard Gardner in his book *Frames of Mind: The Theory of Multiple Intelligences* in 1983.

Gardner surveyed several disciplines and cultures around the world to determine skills and abilities that were deemed to be essential to human development and culture building. He observed candidates on their abilities using eight criteria that must be substantively met by each candidate to justify their identification as an *intelligence*. For Gardner, intelligence is 'a biopsychological potential to process information that can be activated in a cultural setting to solve problems or create products that are of value in a culture'. One model, which to many educators seems to fit with this framework of multiple intelligences, is Bloom's taxonomy, where each intelligence can be outlined along different levels, ranging from basic knowledge up to their highest levels of analysis/synthesis.[132]

The theory of multiple intelligences proposes that individuals possess different types of intelligences, each representing a unique way of processing information and solving problems.

Gardner initially identified seven intelligences:

1. **Linguistic intelligence:** Relates to sensitivity to language, words and communication.
2. **Logical-mathematical intelligence:** The ability to reason logically, analyse problems and think abstractly.
3. **Spatial intelligence:** The capacity to perceive and manipulate visual-spatial information.

4. **Musical intelligence:** Relating to sensitivity to rhythm, melody, pitch and timbre.
5. **Bodily-kinaesthetic intelligence:** The ability to control body movements and handle objects skilfully.
6. **Interpersonal intelligence:** Understanding and interacting effectively with others.
7. **Intrapersonal intelligence:** Related to self-awareness, self-understanding and introspection.

Gardner later proposed additional intelligences under this theory, such as **naturalistic intelligence** (sensitivity to nature and the environment) and **existential intelligence** (contemplation of the 'big questions' of life).

In *Frames of Mind* and its sequels, Gardner stated that these intelligences can be expressed in everyday life in a variety of ways, often referred to as domains, skills, competencies or talents. One model integrates the eight intelligences with Sternberg's Triarchic Theory, whereby each intelligence is actively expressed in three ways: creative, academic/analytical and practical thinking. The two intelligences that are most associated with the traditional perception of general intelligence are the *linguistic* and *logical-mathematical* intelligences. Some intelligence models also include *visual-spatial* intelligence as a third element. Gardner suggests that intelligence is not a single, fixed entity but rather a set of multiple distinct abilities or intelligences. Furthermore, the theory of multiple intelligences observes that individuals exhibit varying strengths and weaknesses across the different intelligences. Some may excel in linguistic and logical-mathematical intelligence, while others may demonstrate strengths in bodily-kinaesthetic or musical intelligence.

The theory of multiple intelligences is known to have several implications for pedagogical strategies for teaching:

- Instructions given to students should be differentiated to accommodate the diverse range of intelligences and learning styles.
- Teachers to use a variety of instructional methods and activities to engage students across different intelligences.
- Assessments should be broad and varied. This will allow students to demonstrate their understanding and skills through different modalities of intelligence.
- Teachers should create a supportive learning environment that values and respects each student's unique strengths and intelligences.[133]

The following segments will help explain the above guidelines in further detail.

SEGMENT A

Instructions given to students should be differentiated to accommodate the diverse range of intelligences and learning styles.

Differentiated instruction involves teaching in a way that is able to meet the different needs and interests of students using varied course content, activities and assessments. It is the attempt to teach *differently* to different students, rather than maintain a one-size-fits-all approach to instruction.[134]

Use of multiple resources to teach the same topic can help in differentiated instruction. Use of illustrations, pictures, tables, charts, graphs and audiovisual material can greatly help in learning. Also, teachers can design activities that involve interaction with peers, family members, etc. This would help learners in not only collecting the required information but also develop their discussion and questioning skills.[135]

Topic: Jainism and Buddhism

Let us take a look at the following activities on the given topic to understand how differentiated instructions work in classrooms.

1. Lecture method: The lecture method is a traditional and widely used teaching strategy in which an educator delivers a structured presentation of information to a large number of students. This approach is centred around the teacher's verbal delivery skill and is often supplemented by visual aids like slides, diagrams and videos.[136]

   For us, the concept of Jainism and Buddhism can be first explained by teachers using the lecture method. Teachers to ask students about their prior knowledge about the topic, then extend the discussion into the historical context of the topic, and finally, explore the various nuances of these religions and their teachings. Teachers can also use PowerPoint presentations and documentaries to help students learn the topic. Thus, by incorporating visual, aural and verbal teaching strategies, the teacher is able to adopt the concept of differentiated instruction.

2. At the end of the lecture/lesson, teachers can quickly conduct a formative assessment to understand the level of content absorption among the students. This can also be differentiated.

   Using popsicle sticks: This helps in getting verbal inputs about the learning levels. For this activity, teachers to put the names of each student on a popsicle stick in a jar or box, kept on the teacher's desk. The student whose name gets pulled from the bundle has to answer a short question based on the day's learning. Knowing their name could be pulled makes the students alert and encourages them to focus on the learning. It also helps the students to verbally articulate their understanding of the content.

   One-minute write-up: This can be used along with other formative assessments to continue with the strategy of differentiation. At the end of a lesson, teachers to give students one minute to write as much as they can about what they learned through the lesson or unit. To make it a bit more engaging, teachers can consider letting students do this with a partner. This way, students are tapping into their linguistic and interpersonal skills. If needed, students can be provided with some guiding questions to get them started.

- What was the most important learning from today, and why?
- Did anything surprise you? If so, what?
- What was the most confusing part of the lesson, and why?
- What is something that will likely appear on a test or quiz, and why?[137]

3. For summative assessments, too, a differentiated approach can be used. Worksheets with visual inputs can be accompanied by projects/exhibitions.

An example of the former is given below. Such continuation of differentiated teaching-learning strategies helps students to have a more comprehensive attitude towards learning.

Question: Study pictures of Jain and Buddhist paintings and answer the following questions:

a. What common motifs do we find in all these sources?
b. What, according to you, are the themes of each of these sources that the artists wanted to express through their work?
c. Do we find any similarities or differences between Buddhist and Jain paintings?

Question: Study sources 4, 5 and 6 and answer the following questions:

a. Write briefly about what you know about these monuments.
b. Identify any three architectural features and briefly discuss them in your answer.

Source 1: The Great Stupa at Sanchi[138]

Source 2: A chaitya in Ajanta Caves[139]

Source 3: Jain Temple, Dilwara[140]

Along with the use of the traditional format of questions and answers, even when we have diversified it with the use of sources, we can use projects/exhibitions as a part of our summative assessments. In the field of education, the term **exhibition** refers to projects, presentations or products through which students 'exhibit' what they have learned, usually as a way of demonstrating whether and to what extent they have achieved the expected learning standards or learning objectives. An exhibition can be both a learning experience in itself and a means of evaluating academic progress and achievement.

In contrast to traditional approaches to assessment, an exhibition may take a wide variety of forms in schools:

1. Oral presentations, speeches or recitation of poems
2. Video-based documentaries, multimedia presentations, audio recordings or podcasts
3. Art, illustration, music, drama, dance or performance
4. Use of print or online publications, including websites or blogs
5. Display of essays, poems, short stories or plays
6. Galleries comprising print or digital photography
7. Presentation of scientific experiments, studies and reports
8. Use of physical products, such as models, sculptures, dioramas, musical instruments or robots.[141]

Thus, by its very nature, such projects or exhibitions work towards differentiated learning. A similar kind of emphasis is found in the multimodal learning theory. It is also referred to as CTML – the 'cognitive theory of multimedia learning' – and focuses on how we learn in an age of screen-based technologies. According to this theory, we primarily learn through two 'channels': aural and visual. To help teachers, Richard Mayer proposed a few strategies that are ideal for teaching using technology:

- **Coherence Principle:** We learn better when extraneous, irrelevant words and images are removed.
- **Signalling Principle:** Learning occurs better when the content is effectively organized and hints are provided to show students the organizational structure.
- **Spatial Contiguity Principle:** Words and images that correspond with each other when placed close together help in learning.
- **Segmenting Principle:** To prevent cognitive overload, knowledge should be presented in small, manageable portions.
- **Pre-Training Principle:** Students learn better when they are prepared for the learning content with some preparatory homework or background knowledge.
- **Modality Principle:** It is believed that graphics and narrations help students learn better than animations alongside on-screen text.
- **Multimedia Principle:** We learn better from images alongside words than from images alone.
- **Personalization Principle:** Conversational style of language is easier to understand and learn from than formal style of language. This approach is also more engaging.
- **Voice Principle:** Human voices help people learn far better than non-human mechanical voices. The human element is essential in the teaching-learning process.[142]

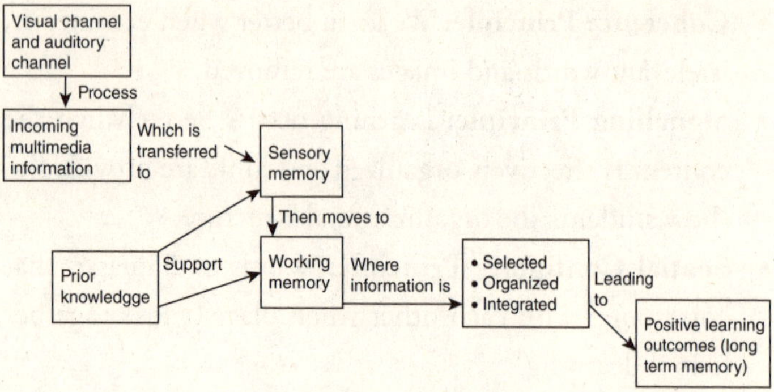

Fig 10: Model of multimodal learning theory[143]

SEGMENT B

Teachers to use a variety of instructional methods and activities to engage students across different intelligences. How much a student is able to remember the content of a sequence of learning activities depends to a large extent on the combination and variety of activities used by the teacher. Children enjoy novelty and need to be exposed to a variety of experiences for optimal and effective learning outcomes. Multiple learning experiences help students to recall and also differentiate between different learning activities.[144]

One of the current challenges pointed out by the National Curriculum Framework, 2023 is that 'Social Science is usually taught as a subject with predominantly rote learning of facts like dates in history, names of geographical features across the globe, the listing of fundamental rights and duties, and naming of economic institutions. The understanding of concepts is often missing in Social Science classrooms. This in turn makes students lose interest in the subject as there are too many facts that are expected to be learnt without adequately engaging with the reasons behind learning them or the core concepts underlying those facts.'[145] Use of a variety of activities will surely make the students interested and also help teachers in tapping into multiple intelligences of the learners.

Method/Activity 1: Poster making (Visual-Spatial Intelligence)

A poster can be explained as a visual tool to communicate information. A poster should be:

FOCUSED: The focus should be on a single message, which will help the audience to remember the main message of the poster. The main message will need to be consistently present throughout the design of the poster. Also, the title has to be easy to read.

SIMPLE: The poster needs to be free from too much information, pictures and graphics. The audience has to be kept in mind and the message should get across to as many different people as possible, like parents, teachers, friends and the whole community. The language and images used should be simple and clear.

COLOURFUL: Use of colours and visual balance will make the poster easier to comprehend.[146]

Topic: Unpacking gender roles.

Approximate duration: 40 minutes

Instructions and variations:

1. Students to work in small groups and identify the common gender roles assigned to women and men.
2. Next, they will need to come up with a few 'breakaways' (roles/activities that do not conform to these conventional gender roles).
3. Students to then come up with posters choosing either one such change or multiple changes in the form of a poster and analyse why and in what ways gender roles are changing in society.
4. As a part of the final step, the groups can then present their work in the class and take part in discussions based on their work.

Research and fact-finding from lived experiences help in a better understanding of the topic. Visual representation in the form of a poster will further help in knowledge accumulation.

Method/Activity 2: Dramatization, Role Play (Bodily-Kinaesthetic Intelligence)

This is one of the most effective methods of stimulating students in their learning journey. It is an organic way by which students freely express their understanding of the life around them. The method allows for a great deal of involvement and participation by the students physically, emotionally and mentally. In a situation where a lesson or topic is dry, dramatization could effectively help to sustain the students' attention and interest. Dramatization involves direct and simple techniques, such as miming plays and role-playing, which can be allocated for such techniques. The teacher could engage students who are less active in academic work. This opportunity would create a sense of belonging in them. The teacher must make adequate preparation to allow the participants to know what part to play. The drama to be staged must rely a good deal on the realistic imagination of the students to make it effective and relevant. Unfortunately, this imagination may sometimes be too realistic to be relevant. While student-written plays are useful and often the most important part of the exercise, they do take up a lot of time, which the teacher may feel is not justified. Nevertheless, dramatization provides, among other things, an avenue for respecting the opinion of others, the attitude of cooperation among the co-actors, the development of desirable skills, confidence and self-esteem, and the opportunity for students to express themselves freely. Students can be led to dramatize the function of a family, the role of the father or mother, honesty, leadership, followership, etc., which are topics in the social studies syllabus.[147]

Topic: Unpacking gender roles.

Activity

Approximate duration: 10 minutes per group

1. Students can be organized into groups by the teacher, with a given topic. Students can then come up with a storyline and screenplay with roles for multiple students as actors, narrators, etc.

2. For 'unpacking gender roles', such skits will be very useful to tap into human emotions and reach out to other students, who can be in the audience.
3. This activity also helps students to work in groups and collaborate with one another.

Method/Activity: Extempore (Verbal-Linguistic Intelligence)

Verbal-linguistic intelligence refers to the capacity to understand the various nuances of written and spoken language. A person with high levels of verbal-linguistic intelligence is able to comprehend and verbally explain things effectively. Teachers use verbal-linguistic skills to communicate information and help students learn on a daily basis. This use of our abilities to convey information and explain concepts to students is vital for the teaching-learning process.[148] Extempore, discussed below, is one method, among many, which can be used to inculcate this skill of verbal-linguistic intelligence among students.

Extempore is seen to assist students in not only thinking on their feet but also in voicing their creative ideas with precision. Extempore is an impromptu speech that is delivered with little or no preparation. Even though this speech is spontaneous, it requires great effort to deliver an extemporaneous speech successfully.

In a course titled 'Oral Communication Skills', offered in a business school, extempore was used as one of the methods to enhance the oral communication skills of students studying management. The group of around 104 students was first told about the nuances of extempore, like the preparation, the process and the dos and don'ts. The students were then given a practise session, based on which they were prompted to work upon their areas of weakness. Personalized feedback was given to each one of them based on their performance during the practise sessions. Extempore was then used to evaluate the oral communication skills of the students.

Each student was given two topics with an option to speak on one of those. Topics were selected from diverse areas, ranging from political and social issues to hypothetical situations to general awareness. Students were then evaluated on a point scale of 25, with the following distribution:

Content: 10 points (topic clarity and logic – 5 each.)

Expression: 10 points (pitch and voice modulation and accuracy – 3 each, language – 4)

Body Language: 5 points (eye contact and gestures – 2 each, facial expressions – 1)

The findings of this activity are quite significant. The overall evaluation of the students proved that around 38 per cent students had very good extempore skills; about 59 per cent of them were good at it, and only about 3 per cent of students fell in the category in which there needed to be an improvement of understanding of extempore skills.

A six-item survey was also created to understand students' perceptions about extempore. The following are the findings:

- 83 per cent of students agreed with the statement that extempore is an effective way to improve communication skills.
- 88 per cent of students accepted that extempore helped boost confidence.
- 93 per cent of students believed that it assisted in managing time.
- 62 per cent felt that the duration for extempore should be two to three minutes.
- Only13 per cent of students found it very easy to give an extempore speech.
- 93 per cent of students felt that the topic played a vital role in extempore.

Extempore, thus, is a good way to practise oral communication skills, which go a long way in boosting the confidence levels of students. It helps in forming wholesome individuals who can think on their feet and can resort to wise but quick action.[149]

Topic: Global Warming (Geography)

Activity

Duration: 10 minutes for preparation, 2–3 minutes for speech

Instructions:

1. Teachers can write down in chits various subtopics and questions that the students can choose from. Examples of such subtopics: 'Are people to blame for

global warming?', 'To reduce carbon footprint, a carbon tax should be established'; 'Is reforestation efficient in reducing global warming?';[150] 'Can cloud seeding help combat global warming? etc.

2. Students can be given ten minutes to think and research on their subtopics individually.
3. Extempore speech needs to be timed. Judging criteria can be the ones already discussed above.

Method/Activity: Plantation Drive (Interpersonal Intelligence)

Topic: Global Warming (Geography)

Interpersonal intelligence can be described as the ability to discover, understand and interpret the desires and intentions of other people, thus allowing for effective social interactions. This intelligence can lead to greater adaptation to the environment, as well as the development of satisfactory social relationships. Since interpersonal intelligence promotes understanding and communication with others, considering their emotions, mood, motivations and intentions, possession of this ability can often become crucial in human societies.

Some of the basic characteristics of people with interpersonal intelligence are the following:

- They are seen to be interested in understanding human reasons and motivations that exist behind different behaviours and reactions. They have a high capacity for analysis and critical thinking.

- Another characteristic is good intuition in the social area through observation and reflection of social relationships.
- Communication is very important to interpersonal intelligence, which is why people tend to be good communicators with good control of speech and non-verbal language, making them able to manage and influence another person effectively.
- They are often able to mediate in times of conflict. Interpersonal intelligence allows a person to understand in the most objective way possible the different points of view, motivations and needs of others, which is why people usually play the role of mediation satisfactorily.
- Such people are also able to maintain old relationships since they take great care of relationships and details and are sensitive to different needs.
- They also have high listening ability. They like to talk with other people, taking into account their points of view and trying to understand them. This active listening helps them in getting to know people and encourages acting coherently with them in the future.
- They enjoy collaborative and social projects since they feel interested in human and social aspects, as well as the intercultural and individual differences of people. People with interpersonal intelligence are also at ease in relating to people of different ages, being able to adjust their behaviour when interacting with them.

- They also have the ability to establish new social relationships, given their orientation towards people and ease of developing healthy and satisfying social ties .[151]

What is a plantation drive?

A plantation drive is a campaign or initiative to promote the planting of trees, usually in a particular area. Whether increasing the tree cover in an area, improving the environment or ecology of the area, or providing economic benefits like employment, the goals of a plantation drive may vary. Planting trees can help to improve the quality of air and water in a region, as well as reduce stormwater run-off and provide habitat for other units of the ecosystem.[152]

Tree planting has become a cornerstone of many environmental campaigns in recent years. The call to plant trees is everywhere, seen as a simple and effective way to help reduce the impact of carbon emissions and restore natural ecosystems, thus helping in combating the ill effects of global warming. Perhaps the most prominent example is the 1 Trillion Trees Campaign launched by the World Economic Forum in Davos in January 2020 in support of the UN's Decade of Ecosystem Restoration. The UN declaration aims to restore, protect or plant one trillion trees by 2030. There are similar campaigns that aim to plant one trillion trees by 2050 , like the one started in 2018 by nature non-profit organizations, including the World Wildlife Fund (WWF).[153]

Such drives need the cooperation of large groups of people, often going beyond one particular organization, for instance, a school. They need interpersonal intelligence from not just students but also teachers who wish to work in a certain neighbourhood. Getting support from parents, the neighbourhood and working closely with authorities will enable the students to assess how well-equipped they are with interpersonal communications.

On a smaller scale, plantation drives can take the form of gifting plant saplings to all members of a school community and urging them to make the world a greener place. Interpersonal intelligence equips our students with the skills needed to navigate the world.

Method/Activity: Active Listening (Musical Intelligence)

Musical intelligence is the ability to capture, assimilate, identify, transform and express forms related to music. This intelligence includes sensitivity to rhythm, as well as tone and timbre. It is believed that musical intelligence is one of the first to develop in a person, right from the time of birth. Babies have the ability to babble and imitate tones and volumes of other people's sounds to the age of two and above, where a child learns different tones and is curious about the sounds they make. Between the fourth and sixth year of life, a clear sensitivity in terms of tones and sounds can be identified.

The following are a few characteristics of musical intelligence that are widely accepted by experts:

- The ability to observe musical forms and recognize different rhythmic patterns.
- The ability to easily learn songs and their rhythms. Generally, people with this intelligence enjoy whistling, humming or singing.
- The ability to identify and distinguish different musical instruments, the tones and notes they produce, as well as to know whether they are out of tune.
- The inclination to play one or more musical instruments.
- The sense of appreciating any sound in the environment, thus being able to capture and distinguish various sounds in the environment, as well as their rhythms and patterns.
- A preference for carrying out activities and tasks with music in the background.
- An ability to express emotions and feelings through music. There is also a sensitivity to capture and understand the emotions that are manifested through the musical medium.
- A marked interest in different musical styles and their evolution, musical culture and the history of music.

Active listening is a type of communication skill that involves going beyond simply hearing the words that another person speaks. It is about actively processing and trying to understand the meaning and intent behind them. Active listening requires being a mindful and focused participant in the communication process.[154]

The benefits of active listening are multiple. Here are a few:

- Helps in building trust.
- Has the capacity to resolve conflicts.
- Broadens a person's knowledge.
- Helps one anticipate problems and prepare for solutions.
- Promotes collaboration and empathy.[155]

When it comes to music, active listening refers to the conscious choice to focus on a piece of music undisturbed by other stimuli. In our daily lives, we may use music as background score, but when we eliminate distractions and focus our attention on the music, we shift into active listening. Active listeners allow themselves to process the compositional structure and nuances in a piece of music. This may help in noticing the different instruments within a particular piece of music or appreciating its complexity.[156]

Let us take a look at an activity in terms of active listening to music to understand the concept better. Our agenda here will be to listen with attention and involvement to different musical compositions and try to identify the instruments that appear, the emotions they produce in you and try to reproduce the rhythms.

Topic: Culture of Medieval India: Carnatic and Hindustani music.

Music piece 1: Raag Reethigowlai (It is a raga in Carnatic music that aims to invoke *bhakti* mixed with immense joy).[157]

Music piece 2: Raga Brindabani Sarang (also known as Raga Sarang, is a Hindustani classical raga depicting the Vrindavan village.)[158]

Can you identify the tone and message of the music to its associated theme? Are you able to recognize a few instruments that may have been used in the performances? What are your general observations on the similarities and differences between Hindustani and Carnatic music?

Let us try and match our experience of active listening to music to the three aspects of active listening discussed by Robin Abrahams and Boris Groysberg from Harvard Business School, in their article 'How to Become a Better Listener':

- Cognitive: Paying attention to all the information, both explicit and implicit, that you are receiving from the other person, while comprehending and integrating that information at the same time.[159] *Paying attention to notes, their changes, tones, the explicit and implicit emotions that they create in us.*
- Emotional: Staying calm and compassionate during the conversation, including managing any emotional reactions (annoyance, boredom) you might experience during the conversation.[160] *Mapping the emotions of ragas has a similar effect when we move from one emotion to the other as expressed by the music.*
- Behavioural: Conveying interest and comprehension verbally and nonverbally.[161] *It is absolutely apparent that*

listening to such ragas needs concentration and focus of attention.

Method/Activity: Critical Thinking (Intrapersonal Intelligence)

Intrapersonal intelligence is the ability to examine, understand and regulate oneself. It is believed to be a critical skill to understanding oneself and predicting human behaviour. Intrapersonal intelligence is necessary for developing capacities involving self-leadership, self-mastery, emotional awareness, self-regulation, self-discipline, intrinsic motivation and other abilities.[162] This category of intelligence can be developed through journaling, introspection, writing and creating mind maps. Such activities are concerned with exploring one's inner thoughts, feelings and mechanisms. Students also need to be encouraged to reflect on their feelings, on lessons taught and putting these thoughts into writing.[163] Critical thinking then becomes a skill that helps a student to develop their intrapersonal intelligence in a great way.

The application of critical thinking includes self-directed, self-disciplined, self-monitored and self-corrective habits of the mind. It is argued that as critical thinking is not a natural process, it must be induced, and ownership of the process must be taken for successful questioning and reasoning. In order to think critically, one needs to overcome biases, egocentrism and other hindrances to logical, analytical reasoning. The use of the phrase 'critical thinking' can be traced to John Dewey, who used the phrase 'reflective thinking', which depends on the knowledge base of an individual. The excellence of critical thinking in which an individual can engage varies according to it.[164]

QUICK FACT

John Dewey[165]

John Dewey was an American philosopher, psychologist, and educational reformer and was one of the most prominent American scholars in the first half of the 20th century. Dewey was also a major educational reformer, a well-known public intellectual and a major voice of progressive education and liberalism. Some of his major works were 'My Pedagogic Creed' (1897), 'The Primary Education Fetish' (1898), *The School and Society* (1900), *The Child and the Curriculum* (1902), *Democracy and Education* (1916), *Schools of To-morrow* [52] (1915) with Evelyn Dewey and *Experience and Education* (1938) among others.

Let us look into a few questions that will make students think critically. The idea here is to give examples of such application-based questions from different topics in social sciences that will help the process of critical thinking.

> No problem can withstand the assault of sustained thinking.
>
> – *Voltaire*[166]

HISTORY

1. The Revolt of 1857
    - What, according to you, was the main reason behind the Revolt of 1857? Explain.
    - To what extent was the defeat of the sepoys due to military reasons?
    - Evaluate the statement: 'The Revolt of 1857 can be considered as the First War of Indian Independence.' Give points for both sides of the argument.
2. The British in India: From Traders to Rulers
    - Discuss the ways in which the economic practices of the Mughal Empire and the European trading companies impacted the course of Indian history.
    - What according to you are the reasons behind India getting colonized by the British?
    - Select any battle fought and won by the East India Company and assess its significance in making the British the rulers of the land in India.

3. The Indian Freedom Struggle
    - What according to you were the major undercurrents of the Indian freedom struggle? Give reasons for your answer.
    - Write about a leader from the Indian freedom struggle who inspires you. Discuss the ways you have applied her/his ideals in your life.
    - Discuss the impact of any one organization connected to the Indian freedom struggle on the movement for freedom.

CIVICS

1. The Constitution of India
    - 'The Preamble manifests in our everyday life.' Discuss with relevant examples.
    - Why do we need a constitution?
    - In what ways does the Constitution of India represent the noble ideas of our freedom fighters?
2. The United Nations
    - What, according to you, are the major benefits of having an international organization like the UN for individual countries?
    - Identify a few global issues and analyse in what ways the UN has affected/impacted these countries.
    - Select any one UN summit and evaluate its success by giving relevant evidence.

GEOGRAPHY

1. Industry
   - To what extent do the industries in developing countries differ from those in developed countries?
   - Why is the sustainable development of industries difficult in less economically developed countries?
   - What are the recent trends in terms of industrial technology? What factors influence the shift in technology?
2. Human Resources
   - Discuss the pros and cons of a population with a majority of young people.
   - In what ways can we turn the human population into a human resource?
   - To what extent does technology replace human labour?

More than just being curious about the world, critical thinkers make connections between logical ideas to see the bigger picture. Building critical thinking skills means being able to advocate one's own ideas and opinions, present them in a logical fashion and make decisions for improvement. It makes a person well-rounded – one who has looked at all their options and possible solutions before making a choice.

According to the University of the People in California, having critical thinking skills is important because these skills are:

- Universal
- Crucial for understanding the economy
- Vital for improving language and presentation skills
- Essential for promoting creativity
- Significant for self-reflection
- Forms the basis of science and democracy

Critical thinking skills differ from individual to individual and are put to use in various ways. Examples of common critical thinking skills include the following:

- Identification of biases: Identifying biases means knowing there are certain people with unfair prejudices or influences on the situation at hand. Pointing out these biases helps to remove them from contention when it comes to solving a problem and allows one to see things from a different perspective.
- Research: Researching details and facts allows one to be prepared when presenting the information to people. Due to the time spent with the subject material during research, one will be well-spoken and know what questions to ask to gain more knowledge. When researching, one should always use credible sources and cross-check factual information.
- Open-mindedness: Being open-minded when having a conversation or participating in a group activity is crucial to critical thinking. Dismissing someone else's ideas before hearing them will inhibit one from progressing to a solution and will often create animosity. One needs

to be willing to hear everyone's opinions and ideas if one wants them to hear their own.

- Analysis: Analysing the research will lead to a better understanding of the elements of the research. As a true critical thinker, one has to seek out the truth and get to the source of issues. It is important to avoid believing information at face value, and one needs to always dig deeper.
- Problem-solving: This is perhaps the most important skill that critical thinkers can come to possess. The ability to solve issues and bounce back from conflict is what helps in succeeding to be a good leader and effect change. One way to properly solve problems is to first recognize there's a problem that needs solving. By determining the issue at hand, one can then analyse it and come up with several potential solutions.[167]

Solving application-based questions gives us further insights into how to think critically and apply our thoughts and solutions to a given problem. By preparing argumentative questions, we inculcate the habit of logical reasoning and give ourselves a better chance of coming to a reasoned conclusion. Rather than putting all our emphasis on fact gathering, we need to strive for application of these very facts in trying to think critically and find a solution – a point made effectively in NEP, 2020, wherein it states that the fundamental principles that need to guide the education system at large are creativity and critical thinking. The ability to make logical decisions and come up with innovative ideas and solutions are vital skills for all learners.[168]

SEGMENT C

Assessments should be broad and varied. This will allow students to demonstrate their understanding and skills through different modalities of intelligence.

Assessments are to gather data that help in understanding the progress and effectiveness of both students' progress and the effectiveness of our teaching programmes. This helps teachers to know what is working well and where they need to make changes.

Formative and summative assessments are the most popular categories and are used widely by teachers around the world. Summative assessments are usually taken at the end of a unit or lesson to determine what students have learned. By doing so, teachers and learners can get a clearer picture of how much progress they have made. Summative assessments are often tests or exams but also include options like essays, projects and presentations. Summative assessments are usually major contributors towards students' report cards.

Formative assessments take place during instruction and are used throughout the learning process to check for understanding and help teachers to make adjustments to instructions and activities as per need. These assessments are not used to calculate grades for students. They are planned as part of a lesson or activity. Teachers use the feedback in terms of results of the formative assessments to determine student progress, both overall and as individuals. If the majority of a class is struggling with a specific concept, the teacher might need to find different ways to teach it. It could also happen that one student is especially falling behind; teachers then need to arrange extra assistance to help her/him out. Including formative assessments in lesson plans by the teacher, at logical points, is very important.[169]

Since formative assessments are varied and more flexible, teachers can use them effectively to evaluate and tap into the multiple intelligences of students. The following are a few examples:

1. Doodle Notes (Visual-Spatial Intelligence)

In 2009, psychologist Jackie Andrade asked 40 people to monitor a two-and-a-half-minute monotonous voicemail message. Half of the group doodled while they did this (they shaded in a shape), and the other half did not. The attendees were not aware that their memories would be tested after the call. Surprisingly, when both groups were asked to recall details from the call, those who doodled were better at paying attention to the message and recalling the details – they recalled 29 per cent more information! Even American presidents have found themselves sketching away: 26 of 44 American Presidents doodled, from Theodore Roosevelt, who was known to doodle animals, to Ronald Reagan, who doodled cowboys and football players, and John F.

Kennedy, who doodled dominoes (quite non-surprisingly!). Traditionally, we have thought of these doodles as a sign of distraction – an indication that your mind was not where it was supposed to be, but recent research has shown that doodling is not an enemy of attention; it may, in fact, be a friend.[170]

Activity

Duration: 15 minutes or more

1. Teachers to assign a set time when students will be allowed to use their doodling skills while listening to an audio clip or instructions from teachers. The activity has to be guided by teachers, who will need to first give students examples of doodles, explain its benefits and also help them get started.
2. The activity can also be done at the end of the class, wherein students can be asked to doodle their thoughts on the topic taught in class.
3. Examples of such topics could be the layers of the atmosphere, lithosphere, the levels of the local self-governments, the provisions of the Morley–Minto reforms, the takeaways of learning about the Non-Cooperation Movement, etc.

2. Four Corners (Verbal-Linguistic and Bodily-Kinaesthetic Intelligences)

This activity can be used with questions or opinions, at the start or even at the end of a lesson. Before asking the question/making the statement, teachers to set each corner of the classroom as a different potential opinion or answer. After giving the prompt, each student goes to the corner that best represents their answer. This is followed by a classroom discussion, wherein students can have the option to move from corner to corner, adjusting their answer or opinion.[171]

Activity

Duration: 10 minutes or more

1. Teachers to set a question or make a statement. For example: 'What made the British to finally give India independence in August 1947?'
2. The four corners of the room are then marked as potential opinions or answers. For example: Corner A: Mahatma Gandhi's contribution, Corner B: the huge expenses incurred during World War II made holding onto India by the British expensive, Corner C: the establishment of the United Nations and support for self-determination in the colonies, Corner D: the contributions of other leaders and political parties.
3. Rounds of class discussions can be followed by an option given to students to either stick to their opinions or change to another corner. They will also need to justify their stance.

The Four Corners strategy is a wonderful way to encourage debate and discussion in the classroom while also visualizing students' differences in ideas. By posing questions that have a more open-ended response, teachers can encourage students to think more critically about the questions and their answers and prompt them to justify their choices.[172]

Self-Directed (Intrapersonal Intelligence)

This one can be a little difficult at first for some students, but it can be incredibly powerful to let students themselves choose how they want to demonstrate learning. Teachers can support students by giving them managed choice but let them decide if and how they want to show what they understood as the essential parts of the lesson. This can be done by drawing a picture, writing a paragraph, creating a pop quiz or even writing song lyrics. This puts them in charge of their own learning.

SEGMENT D

Teachers should create a supportive learning environment that values and respects each student's unique strengths and intelligences.

In this context, it is pertinent to discuss two concepts: a student-centric approach and the range of learning experiences.

In a **student-centric approach**, the teaching and learning processes give primacy to and evolve through children's experiences and their active participation. Teachers try to identify concepts, skills and issues/concerns faced by learners and develop appropriate strategies that help them with the understanding. This implies that teachers need to:

1. Provide some flexibility in the classroom to accommodate development along lines of inquiry of the students.
2. Provide opportunities, as well as the necessary resources, to enable students to experiment, explore and discover for themselves.
3. Create an environment where learners feel free to ask questions.[173]

The humanist theory believes that human beings need comforting, welcoming environments for optimal learning to occur. When applied to the field of education, humanism emphasizes two pillars:

- Holistic well-being: An emphasis on the importance of a student's whole well-being, not just their intellectual knowledge.
- Choice-based approach: This gives children a sense that they have control over their lives and treats this choice as highly important in education.[174]

QUICK FACT

One of the most significant scholars when it comes to the humanist theory for educators is Abraham Harold Maslow. Maslow developed his hierarchy of needs, which highlights how students will learn best when they feel safe and well cared for. He believed that when a student's basic needs were met, they would be more creative and confident learners. The hierarchy that Maslow discussed can be summarized with the help of the following diagram:

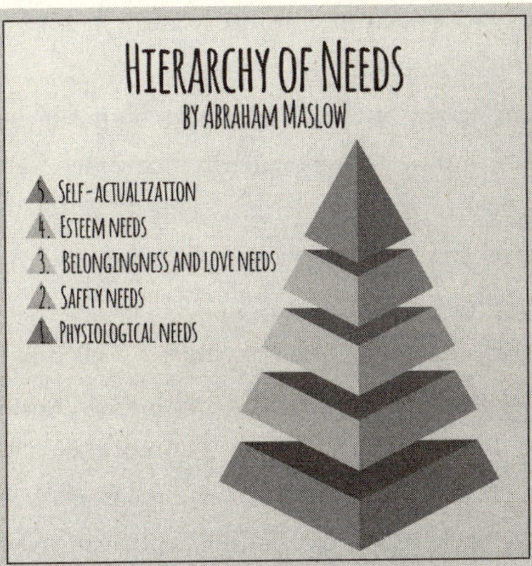

Maslow's hierarchy of needs[175] *Abraham Maslow*[176]

The steps in the hierarchy are as follows:

- Psychological Needs: Learners require their basic needs for survival to be met in order to focus on their learning. Such basic needs can be food, water, clothing and shelter. It is true that a hungry student (or any person) may not have the correct mental space to learn.
- Safety, Protection and Security Needs: A student needs to feel safe when they learn. If a student feels insecure, she/he might get distracted from learning or too anxious to learn.
- Belongingness and Love Needs: When students develop a sense of belonging, they feel more comfortable and happier in their learning space. This leads to more

productive working conditions and effective teaching-learning takes place.

- Esteem Needs: Students who have high self-esteem will be more willing to make an effort and believe that they can succeed. Such students also feel confident to take risks and apply themselves more to participate in the learning journey.
- Self-Actualization: Students who have all their learning needs met are believed to reach self-actualization, which means they become the best version of themselves.

Another central humanist theorist is Carl Rogers. According to Rogers, students have a natural will to learn, which he called the 'actualizing tendency'. As teachers, we need to offer them 'freedom to learn'. Furthermore, Rogers believed that students would perform best when their teacher had strong faith and confidence in their abilities. Rogers claimed that teachers should provide 'unconditional positive regard' to students and need to always see students as capable of self-improvement, even if they've misbehaved all day long. Positive reinforcements, even after a tough day, by the teacher goes a long way in motivating students to give their best in what they do.[177]

The range of learning experiences recognizes different learning styles and individual differences among children. The aim is to ensure that learning is a joyful experience for all children and that they are able to understand not only what they learn but also how this learning is relevant in their lives, both for the present and the future.

Teachers are thus advised to use a range of interesting and engaging activities/tasks that cater to different learning styles, e.g., various strategies, ranging from discussions, role play, hands-on experiences, case studies, field visits, project work, surveys, model making, poster making, slogan writing, etc., may be used.[178]

Using the approaches and concepts discussed above, teachers can use the following activities to create a supportive learning environment that values and respects each student's unique strengths and intelligences.

Slogan Contest

Activity

Duration: 30–40 minutes

1. Teachers to first ask students one issue they think needs immediate action from our society. Topics and themes can be anything that concerns human society (thus, it is a study with a wide range of options for learning. Topics could be as varied as sensitization on the importance of wetlands, saving birds in urban settlements, the importance of perspectives in studying history, concerns over awareness of rights and duties of citizens, etc.)
2. Students can then work in pairs or groups to make posters and come up with slogans that communicate their issue/topic effectively. Slogans need to be short and catchy to grab the attention of onlookers.

3. This activity also helps students to tap into their emotions and can assist them in articulating their opinions and feelings. Thus, it is essential for teachers to create a safe, encouraging learning environment for such activities to be effective.

Traffic Lights

We all know the meaning behind the lights at traffic signals. We usually have a similar kind of idea attached to the colours of the traffic lights in our cognition. The activity below uses this concept of traffic lights, wherein red symbolizes a lack of understanding, yellow stands for partial understanding, and green symbolizes full understanding.

Activity

Duration: 5 minutes

1. At the end of a lesson, academic or a general discussion, teachers can assign small pieces of paper with the image of traffic lights printed on them. Or simply give students Post-it notes, where there are the three colours, red, yellow and green, which are pre-marked.
2. Students are then asked to think about the topic covered in class or any discussion that has taken place (class teachers can use this method to understand the level of awareness for discipline or school rules, etc). Individually, students write down what they have fully understood (besides the green mark), partially understood (beside

the yellow mark) and not understood (beside the red mark)

3. This is submitted to the teacher, who has to maintain confidentiality since this is an activity that requires such sensitivity from educators – children might not feel free to mark out their lack of understanding otherwise.

The connection that teachers have with students is perhaps one of the most genuine and loving relationships known to us. From my personal experience, I can safely say that students perform way better when they feel safe in the presence of their teachers. Whether it is their academic results or performances in extracurricular activities, a teacher who encourages them to give their best will always be someone they feel a connection with. I have this motto as a teacher: I will listen to my students when they want to share. I might not be able to give them a solution, but I can assure them that they can vent out and share their journeys – both the happy turns of events and not-so-happy eventualities, without them being 'scared' or anxious. Of course, strictness is needed at times, for example, adherence to discipline, school rules and instilling good values, but teachers are also encouraged to be gentle while making the students realize and harness their highest potential.

Chapter 6

Constructivism

A group of men who did not have the ability to see came across a strange animal called an elephant. All of them could hear the animal but were unaware of its shape and form. Out of curiosity, they wanted to inspect and learn about it by touching the animal.

The first person, whose hand touched the trunk, felt that the animal was like a thick snake. For another one whose hand reached its ear, the animal seemed to have the form of a fan. As for the third person, whose hand was on its leg, he felt that the elephant was a pillar or a huge tree trunk. The one whose hand was on the side of the elephant imagined the animal to be a big wall. Another who felt its tail described the animal as a rope. The last person felt its tusk, stating the elephant is that which is hard, smooth and like a spear.

The parable is believed to have originated in ancient India, from where it has been widely diffused. The Buddhist text *Tittha Sutta,* dated to around c. 500 BCE, contains one of the earliest versions of the story. Other versions of the parable describe sighted men encountering a large statue on a dark night or some other large object while blindfolded.

This parable has often been used to imply that one's subjective experience can be true but that such an experience is inherently limited by its failure to account for other truths or a totality of the truth.[179]

For us, we might use the same concept to understand Constructivism.

Constructivism is based on the idea that we construct learning new ideas based on our own prior knowledge and experiences. Learning, therefore, is unique to the individual learner. Thus, we can say that for these blind men, their perception of the elephant – like a snake, fan, tree trunk, wall, rope, spear – depends on the prior knowledge of these men. If these men (learners) did not have an idea as to what they were relating the animal with, their version of the animal would not have come to a reasoned conclusion. Similarly, we can argue that students adapt their models of understanding by reflecting on prior theories (prior knowledge).

This can also be done by resolving misconceptions.[180] In some versions of the above-mentioned parable, the blind men then discover their disagreements, suspect the others to be not telling the truth and come to blows.[181] Thus, looking into others' perspectives (agreeing comes in later, if at all it comes in), helps in resolving misconceptions and thus helps learners in 'constructing' knowledge.

Bruner's Spiral Curriculum helps learners to build on their prior knowledge to construct new knowledge.

> *'We begin with the hypothesis that any subject can be taught in some intellectually honest form to any child at any stage of development'.*[182]

In other words, even very complex topics can be taught to learners if structured and presented in the right way.

The spiral curriculum is based on three key ideas.

1. Learners revisit the same topic multiple times throughout their school career, thus reinforcing the learning each time they return to the subject.
2. The complexity of the topic increases each time a learner revisits it. This process allows progression through the subject matter keeping in mind the development of the student's cognitive ability with age.
3. When a student returns to a topic, new ideas are linked with the ones they have already learned. Thus, there is familiarity with the keywords and ideas, which enables them to grasp the more difficult elements of the topic in a stronger way.[183]

Jerome Bruner's spiral curriculum approach not only promoted learning by building on prior knowledge, but it also uses other principles like Cyclical Learning and Increase in Depth on each Iteration.[184] Cyclical learning is a process in teaching and learning where our learning will pass through the same areas of study repeatedly over time, just like we pass through the seasons every year. This way, learning spirals continually deeper with every cycle we are a part of.[185]

To design a curriculum using a spiral approach, teachers need to create units of work that increase in complexity and start off where the previous unit ended. This approach is a reminder that courses are not singular, set-in-stone units of work; instead, each course or unit of work that we cover builds upon something previously covered.

For a successful integration of the spiral approach, we need to work with our colleagues who were a child's teacher in a previous year or in years to come to develop a cohesive approach to teaching. Use of Bloom's Taxonomy can help us with learning outcomes at different stages of a course. Teachers will also need to develop learning outcomes that have increasing levels of complexity. For example, in the first course or unit, a student might only need to demonstrate 'understanding' of the topic. At the next iteration, they may need to 'critique' or 'analyse' the given unit. In the final iteration, the students may need to 'create' something from scratch to demonstrate their learning.[186]

Let us refer to the following example to see how we can use these principles to apply Bruner's spiral curriculum in our social science lessons.

History: In this instance, teachers of two grades (for example, grades 6 and 7) can come together to follow the given spiral curriculum.

Prior Knowledge	Cyclical Learning Instances	Increase in Depth on Each Iteration	Use of Bloom's Taxonomy
The Delhi Sultanate	Babur's invasion of India, First Battle of Panipat	How did power transfer? What made the Mughals different? What was continued under Babur?	Understand
Babur establishes the Mughal Empire in India	Humayun, Sher Shah Suri	Humayun as the successor of Babur, was Sher Shah a better administrator?	Critique
Humayun wins back his empire	Akbar	How did Akbar consolidate what Humayun had won back? Indo-Islamic culture, architecture, paintings, etc	Create
Akbar's policies	Relations with Rajputs, Marathas, etc,	Akbar's policies to consolidate, expand, administer, etc.	Analyse
Mughal emperors till Aurangzeb	Aurangzeb's policies	Changes and continuation – post Akbar.	Evaluate

Aurangzeb and the later Mughals	Decline of the Mughal Empire, arrival of the Europeans in India	Aurangzeb and his policies towards the Rajputs, Marathas, etc. Why the change in policy? Results. European presence in India.	Compare and contrast

Bloom's Taxonomy

Taxonomy, in a broader sense, means the science of classification.[187] Bloom's taxonomy is a framework used to categorize educational goals. This categorization was developed by a committee of educators chaired by Benjamin Bloom in 1956 and was first introduced in the publication *Taxonomy of Educational Objectives: The Classification of Educational Goals*. The taxonomy divides learning objectives into three broad domains:

- cognitive, which is knowledge-based,
- affective, which is emotion-based, and
- psychomotor, which is action-based.

Each category comes with a hierarchy of skills and abilities. These domains are used by teachers and educators to structure curricula, assessments and teaching methods to foster different types of learning.[188]

Advantages and Disadvantages of Bruner's Spiral Curriculum

Advantages	**Disadvantages**
1. Developmentally appropriate learning	1. Time-consuming for designers
2. Prior knowledge is central to learning	2. The curriculum gets crowded
3. Spaced repetition occurs	3. Irrelevant for short courses
4. Teachers focus on structuring work to follow logical progression	4. It risks becoming teacher-centred
5. Integration and collaboration occur	5. Teachers find themselves re-teaching content over and again[189]

We can say that Bruner's approach highlights the open-ended nature of learning and shows how learning is a never-ending lifelong process. While it is widely accepted as an appropriate approach for long-term school curriculum design, it does have limitations. These include the risk that the curriculum becomes too rigid and crowded and that educators will have to focus on re-teaching content that wasn't taught well enough or has been forgotten by learners since the last time the topic was taught.[190]

Continuing with Bloom's Taxonomy, let us now look into some activities that will work towards the three categories of learning objectives as mentioned by Bloom: Cognitive, Affective and Psychomotor

Cognitive:

Report writing

The learning objective based on knowledge acquisition, or in other words, focused on cognition, can be effectively exercised through multiple teaching strategies. One such being report writing. A report is a specific form of writing, written concisely and clearly. It is typically organized around identifying and examining issues, events or findings from a research investigation. Reports often involve investigating and analysing an issue and coming up with a solution. Thus, the cognitive acts of research, critical thinking and writing are all part of this exercise.

How to write a report?

A report should include the following:

- an analysis of existing data and literature
- conducting analysis and problem-solving
- results of an investigation

It is essential for reports to be well-written, clearly structured and expressed in a way that suits the audience. Equally important for a report is the central message, which will help in making the report clear and persuasive.

There are three main phases of report writing, all of which require the use of cognitive structures of the human brain:

The **preparation** phase: Here, one analyses exactly what one is being asked to do, and in case of a group, agreement on the group communication plan needs to be in place.

The **analysis** phase: This comprises gathering all evidence, conducting research, undertaking investigations, completing calculations, etc.

The analysis phase will enable one to come up with the key message – the answer to the question/solution to the problem. This key message will then determine the structure of the report and enable one to complete the **writing** phase of the report.[191]

Activity

Approximate duration: Research work: 20 minutes, Report writing: 20 minutes

1. Teachers can assign individual or groups of students a particular city or town for an air quality inspection report.
2. Students to research using newspapers, magazines, books and the internet for governmental reports and agency findings.
3. If it is possible, survey work can also be undertaken by students with guidance from the subject teacher.
4. After consulting various sources, a report can be made and presented before the class. Use of diagrams, pie charts, etc., can also assist in the representation of the data. Analyses

can draw on points like current air quality markers, reasons, past records, factors influencing air quality of the said region, ways to improve quality, challenges, etc.

See the following examples of tables:

Table 1: Air pollutants in Delhi

Study and year	Variable	Findings
Goyal et al., 2011[(6)]	Indoor air pollution in classrooms close to heavy traffic roads	Vehicle exhaust emissions are the only significant contributor to indoor concentrations of $PM_{2.5}$ and $PM_{1.0}$
Kumar et al., 2009[(7)]	Indoor air lead pollution	Lead loading for floor and interior windowsill samples was 19.7 μg/ft^2 and 75.5 μg/ft^2, respectively
Kumar et al., 2001[(8)]	Outdoor air	Inhalable particulates in the ambient air increased due to industrial activities up to 320,168 and 546%, and due to commercial activities up to 406, 198 and 140% in Ahmedabad, Mumbai and Delhi, respectively. There was seasonal variation also
Balachandran et al., 2000[(9)]	Outdoor air	Coarse PM_{10} - 68.3 ± 17 μg/m^3: fine PM_{10} 71.3 ± 15 μg/m^3. Three major sources were vehicular emissions, industrial emission and soil re-suspension

From S.A. Rizwan, Baridalyne Nongkynrih and Sanjeev Kumar Gupta in 'Air Pollution in Delhi: Its Magnitude and Effects on Health'[192]

Table 2: Effects of air pollution in Delhi on health

Study and year	Variable	Findings
Siddique et al., 2011[20]	Vehicular air pollution effects in children	Ambient PM_{10} level was positively correlated with ADHD in children (OR = 2.07; 95% Cl, 1.08–3.99)
Rajarathnam et al., 2011[23]	Outdoor air	It was found that every 10 µg/m³ change in PM_{10} was associated with 0.15% increase in total all-natural-cause mortality
Kumar et al., 2008[16]	Indoor air pollution	Indoor SO_2, NO_2 and suspended particulate effects in children matter levels were high in houses with family history of smoking. Indoor air pollution was associated with respiratory function of children
Kulshreshtha et al., 2008[16]	Indoor air	High levels of indoor airborne pollutants during winter were associated with respiratory problems for women and children.
Jayaraman, 2008[13]	Outdoor air	10 µg/m³ rise in pollutant level led to statistically significant relative risks (RR) for respiratory morbidity: 1.033 for O_3, 1.004 for NO_2, 1.006 for RSPM

Study and year	Variable	Findings
Nidhi et al., 2007[(24)]	Outdoor air	The relative risks of hospitalization due to respiratory diseases were 1.07–2.82
Kumar, 2007[(19)]	Indoor air pollution	Indoor SPM level also significantly effects in children higher in homes of children with a history of respiratory illness
Agarwal et al., 2006[(12)]	Outdoor air	SPM ($r = 0.474$; $P < 0.01$) and RSPM ($r = 0.353$: $P < 0.05$) showed a significant positive correlation with the number of COPD cases. Winter months had higher risk
Pande et al., 2002[(25)]	Outdoor air	Emergency room visits for asthma, COAD and acute coronary events increased by 21.30%, 24.90% and 24.30%, respectively, due to higher than acceptable levels of air pollutants

From S.A. Rizwan, Baridalyne Nongkynrih, and Sanjeev Kumar Gupta in 'Air Pollution in Delhi: Its Magnitude and Effects on Health'[193]

The VARK Modalities Theory, developed by Fleming and Mills in 1992, states that reading/writing learners prefer to learn through written words. While there is some overlap with visual learning, learners with this type of learning preference are drawn to expression through writing, reading articles or books, writing in diaries, looking up words in the dictionary and searching the internet for just about everything. Students with this learning style want to absorb information through the written word, and as teachers, we need to give them plenty of opportunities to get their ideas out on paper.[194]

QUICK FACT

The VARK modalities theory states that the four modalities – visual, aural, reading/writing and kinaesthetic – are used for learning information. These sensory modalities, although with some overlap between them, seem to reflect the experiences of both students and teachers. The acronym VARK stands for these four modalities.[195]

Affective

Podcast

Podcasts have become one of the most popular forms of digital media. There is a staggering number of new episodes published to podcast directories every day. Podcasts are a collection or series of digital audio files that are made available for downloading or listening via the internet. Each individual audio recording is called a podcast episode. Podcasts are generally hosted by an individual or individuals who lead a conversation, share stories, conduct interviews or report the news. The person creating a podcast is known as a podcaster. Podcasting has increasingly become a conveniently accessible medium for both listeners and creators worldwide.

With the present advancement in technology, podcasters interested in creating their own podcasts have several avenues to publish their work. Unlike radio stations and television networks, which are often subject to regulations and approvals, several podcasting platforms allow for self-publishing.[196] However, judgement of what is valuable and needs discussion is a responsibility of great significance. Equally vital is the adherence to decorum, especially for podcasters catering to young audiences.

For listeners, a podcast operates like an on-demand internet radio show. One can listen to episodes on a podcast app or subscribe to podcasts online, and subscribers are often notified each time a new episode is available. Nowadays, most smartphones come equipped with a media player, which allows one to subscribe to podcasts and stream or download podcast episodes at their convenience.

Types of Podcasts

1. **Scripted fiction**: These are audio-only theatrical productions, and some might tell a single serialized story, like a TV show or audiobook. They may tell a new story with each episode.
2. **Interview**: These podcasts generally have a host or a pair of co-hosts who conduct an interview with a person of interest. A format similar to that of a TV talk show can be followed.

3. **Monologue**: In these, a single individual can produce a monologue. The podcaster might be an expert in a particular field with information to share, a storyteller, comedian or news anchor.
4. **Non-fiction storytelling**: This has become one of the most popular types of podcasts. In these storytelling podcasts, true stories can be retold and may contain interviews with those involved in the story or an expert with knowledge of the story.
5. **Conversational**: Another popular podcast format involves a panel of hosts who record themselves having interesting conversations on a specific topic. Themes for such podcasts can be varied, often including topics on sports, pop culture, science, history and more.[197]

In order to use podcasts for affective learning objectives, teachers need to assign a topic that needs emotion-based learning. Such topics can be varied: 'What freedom means to you?'; 'Should the voting age be lowered in India?'; 'Can economic development at the cost of the environment be a good decision?' etc. The following activity is an example of how teachers can use this strategy to promote affective learning.

Approximate duration: 30–40 minutes

Instructions and variations:

1. Teachers can assign certain topics, like 'Ways to protect our environment', to groups of students.

2. Next, working in groups, students to research the given topic and come up with a script that can be read out during the podcast.
3. Inspiration can be taken from podcasts available on the internet that cover similar topics. The BBC Earth Podcast 'Defenders of the Earth' can be a starting point for the research.[198]
4. Students to keep in mind that for affective learning, the idea is to tap into human emotions and base our study on learning these emotions. So, critical thinking on the lines of what a good environment means for us, how we benefit from environmental health, economic and social consequences of unhygienic living conditions, how we motivate others to work for the betterment of our environment and other such related questions need to addressed and discussed during the podcast.
5. The final version of the podcasts, after being reviewed by teachers, can be put up on common sharing sites that are allowed by the respective institutions for all students and teachers to listen to in their free time.

Podcasts can help auditory learners in a great way. Auditory learners tend to learn better when the subject matter is reinforced by sound. Students with this kind of learning preference would much rather listen to a lecture than read written notes. Auditory learners often use their own voices to reinforce new concepts and ideas, and they prefer reading out loud to themselves. They are generally not afraid to speak up in class and are great at verbally explaining things![199]

How to Create a Podcast

To create a podcast, one needs a few pieces of equipment, such as a USB microphone, pop filter and headphones.[200] A pop filter, also known as a pop shield or pop screen, is a noise protection filter for microphones. It is generally used in a recording studio and serves to reduce or eliminate the popping sounds caused by the mechanical impact of fast-moving air on the microphone during recorded speech.[201] Access to audio recording and editing software to produce one's own audio content is also an important requisite.[202]

Psychomotor

Dramatization and Role Play

In psychomotor learning, the focus is on the relationship between cognitive functions and physical movement. It is believed that psychomotor learning is demonstrated by physical skills like movement, coordination, manipulation, dexterity, grace, strength and speed–actions that demonstrate the fine or gross motor skills. These gross motor skills include the use of precision instruments or tools, walking, etc. Sports and dance are thought to be the richest realms of gross psychomotor skills.[203]

Drama is considered to be a multifaceted teaching approach that encompasses cognitive, moral, linguistic, emotional and motor growth. It prepares learners to understand the underlying gravity of social issues and helps them develop their problem-solving skills, which they can use in real-life situations. In drama education, we find a holistic way of learning, which involves a wide range of expressions in the form of dance, music, painting, performing arts, visual arts, crafts work, self-expression and animation – to name a few.[204]

Rudraprasad Sengupta, whose group Nandikar, an institution that has been at the forefront of the national theatre movement since its inception in 1960 with its logo designed by Satyajit Ray, has consistently expressed the importance of drama in education, especially at the school level.[205] In an interview in 2010, Mr Sengupta observed '... School education is incomplete unless drama is incorporated within the curriculum because that is the only way in which both the mind and the body are at work together, which teach the child the use of all the five senses. That is essential for a child's development...'[206]

Dramatization Method as Pedagogy:

This is one of the most effective methods to stimulate students in their learning journey. It is an organic way by which learners freely express their understanding of the life around them. The method allows for the involvement and participation of students, physically, emotionally and mentally. In a situation where a lesson or topic is prone to monotony, dramatization could be especially effective to help sustain students' attention and interest.

Dramatization involves direct and simple techniques such as role-playing.[207]

The teacher must prepare adequately to allow the participants to first think and write a script (if it is to be authored by the students) or select a play that adheres to a given theme. When learners are involved in rehearsals and the enactment of a skit, play or act, they are actively tapping into their psychomotor skills, which help them in learning by doing.

Activity: Play on the Indian National Movement

Approximate duration: 40 minutes

Instructions and variations:

1. Teachers to guide the students as to which areas they can focus on. In groups, they can look into different phases and events of the Indian national movement. The focus can be on enactments of topics like the Dandi March, Declaration of Poorna Swaraj, the Quit India Movement, etc., or can be an enactment of speeches by national leaders, for example, Netaji Subhas Chandra Bose's speech 'Give me blood, and I shall give you freedom', Jawaharlal Nehru's speech 'Tryst with destiny', etc.
2. Teachers to look into the historical accuracy of the scripts thus produced by students and assist them in developing their plays.

3. Enactments can be done in front of a small audience (for classmates) or performed as part of school assemblies.

Such learning by doing works brilliantly for all students, especially learners whose preferred learning style is kinaesthetic.

Kinaesthetic learners, also known as tactile learners, prefer to learn through experiencing or doing things. They learn by getting involved, by acting out events. Young learners with this learning preference also like to use their hands to touch and handle to understand concepts. They may struggle to sit still and often excel at sports or dance, which gives them opportunities to move and learn. They may often need to take frequent breaks while studying.[208]

Till now, we have covered three types of learning preferences: reading/writing, auditory and kinaesthetic. The other most common learning type is visual learners. Students with a preference for visual learning are partial to seeing and observing things, including pictures, diagrams, written directions and more. This learning style is also referred to as the 'spatial' learning style. Students who learn through sight understand information better when it's presented in a visual way. Visual learners are your doodling students, your list-makers and your students who take notes.[209]

Activity: Mind map as a tool for visual learners.

Mind map, as developed by Tony Buzan, is a note-taking technique that can be considered as an application with the power of uncovering the thoughts of the brain about a subject from different viewpoints. This technique also helps in activating the right and left lobes of the brain together as an alternative to linear thought. It is observed that mind maps have benefits such as recalling, improving creativity, solving problems, focusing on a subject and organizing the thoughts of learners. Mind maps have an important place as a lifelong learning tool and are vital for the learning-teaching process.

Tony Buzan emphasizes four important features of mind maps:

- Attention to the subject could be provided by a picture at the centre of the mind map.
- Main themes and criteria of the subject are designed in the form of branches related to the picture at the centre.
- Branches state a key picture or keyword using the connected lines.
- Branches have a structure that is related to the other branches.[210]

T. Steyn and A. Boer, in their studies, concluded that learners enjoy using the mind map technique and remember easily what they learned with the help of this technique. K. Goodnough and R. Woods are of the opinion that students express positive opinions about mind mapping and find this technique interesting and enjoyable.[211] And since the information on mind maps is represented visually, it becomes an important learning tool for all visual learners.

Activity: Mind maps can be a useful tool in collating multiple categories of information into comprehensive, effective study material. Let us see how we can use mind maps to study the Revolt of 1857.

Approximate duration: 20–30 minutes

1. Teachers to assign a segment of the given topic, like 'Reasons for the Revolt of 1857' or 'Results of the Revolt', and ask students to categorize their points and represent them using the blank mind map provided below.
2. Alternatively, digital mind maps can be created online as well.
3. Once finished, students can take turns to explain their work to the rest of the class, or these maps can simply be put up for all the students to observe and learn from each other.

Theories of learning styles emphasize that different learners have different approaches to learning and thus require educators to reflect on the importance of differentiation: teaching the same content in different ways for different types of learners.[212] The learning-styles view has acquired great influence within the field of education and is frequently seen to operate at levels ranging from kindergarten to graduate school.[213] However, scholars like Frank Coffield highlight that there is very little scientific evidence for learning-styles theories and believe that we do not have inherent learning styles from birth but what we can have are **learning**

preferences. Personal preferences can emerge through our own lives rather than as inherited, in-built mental structures that make us learn better in some ways than others.[214]

Catering to different learning patterns can be challenging for teachers, who are often likely to be overwhelmed with work. It can also test the limits of the available resources of an institution. One solution to this issue has been proposed by the Centre for Applied Special Technology (CAST), which works towards creating a global community to design equitable, inclusive learning experiences through the Universal Design for Learning (UDL) framework.[215]

Universal Design Learning: It is a framework that aims to improve and optimize teaching and learning for all, based on scientific insights into how humans learn. The UDL Guidelines 3.0 states the following:

> '**Engagement** is one of the guiding Principles of the UDL. A learner's interests and sources of motivation may vary depending on the context, with some learners highly engaged by spontaneity and novelty while others are disengaged, and even frightened, by those aspects. Instead, preferring strict routine. In another instance, a learner might like to work alone, while others prefer to work with their peers. And these learning preferences might vary from week to week or even day to day. As such in reality, there is not one means of engagement that will be

optimal, effective for all learners in all contexts. Multiple options for engagement are essential.

Multiple means of **Representation** are necessary since learners differ in the ways they perceive and make meaning of information. For example, those with sensory disabilities (e.g., blindness or deafness), learning disabilities (e.g., dyslexia), and those representing diverse or non-dominant cultures and/or languages all approach content differently. These differing approaches must be honored and valued. Equally important is the consideration of how people, cultures, individual and collective identities, perspectives, and ways of knowing are represented within the content. Learning, and transfer of learning, occurs when multiple representations, perspectives are used, because they support learners to make connections within, as well as between, concepts. In short, there is not one means of representation that will be optimal for every learner. Teachers need to provide multiple options for representation.

It is also essential to design for and honor the varying forms **of action and expression.** Learners differ in the ways they navigate a learning environment and express what they know. Depending on the context, some may prefer to express themselves in

> written text but not speech, and vice versa and as such, it should also be recognized that action and expression require a great deal of strategy, practice, and organization, and this is another area in which learners will differ. In reality, there is not one means of action and expression that will be effective for every learner. Options for action and expression are essential.[216],

Understanding different learning styles doesn't end in the classroom. An awareness of how a child learns best can dramatically affect their ability to connect with the topics we are teaching, as well as how they participate with the rest of the class. The role of parents in a child's education is crucial, and positive parental involvement in education will further enhance a child's learning experience, fostering academic success and overall development.[217]

Chapter 7

National Education Policy 2020

At the Heads of State and Government and High Representatives meeting at the United Nations headquarters in New York in September 2015, a set of 17 new global Sustainable Development Goals were decided. These new goals and targets came into effect on 1 January 2016 and will guide policymakers throughout the world over the next 15 years.

One of the new goals' aims is to 'commit to providing inclusive and equitable quality education at all levels – early childhood, primary, secondary, tertiary, technical and vocational training'.[218]This Goal 4 (SDG4) of the 2030 Agenda for Sustainable Development has been instrumental in shaping India's drive towards a new National Education Policy. India has pledged to 'ensure inclusive and equitable quality education and promote lifelong learning opportunities for all' by around 2025[219] – a similar year mark (2030) has been targeted by the UN SDG as well. The experts behind the NEP expect to bring about a long-lasting, positive impact on the education system in India and make the country a global hub of skilled manpower.

The next 25 years leading up to a developed India in 2047 has been termed 'Amrit Kaal'.[220]

The NEP 2020 is known to have been founded on the five guiding pillars of **Access, Equity, Quality, Affordability and Accountability.** It is to prepare the youth of the country to meet the diverse national and global challenges of the present and the future.[221] In its fundamental principles, the policy recognizes the need for full equity and inclusion in our education system. It should be the cornerstone of all educational decisions to ensure that all learners achieve their full potential. For achieving social justice and equality, we need to have an education system that aims to give all children the opportunity to learn and excel, despite any hindrances caused by circumstances of birth or background.[222] The SDG4 also reflects similar targets when it states that by 2030, the world needs to work together to eliminate gender disparities in education and ensure equal access to all levels of education and vocational training. This is especially true for providing such opportunities to the vulnerable, including differently-abled people, indigenous people and children in vulnerable situations. The UN, through the SDG, also aspires to increase the number of youth and adults who have relevant skills, including technical and vocational skills, for increased employment, decent jobs and the creation of entrepreneurship.[223]

One very important point to be noted is the steady decline of overall enrolments in Indian schools from grade

1 to grade 12. This declining enrolment is significantly more pronounced for many of the SEDGs (Socio-Economically Disadvantaged Groups). This is ever more evident in the steep decline in female students' enrolment and often even steeper in higher education.[224] This area of concern also gets intense attention in SDG4, whereby it states that a) by 2030, we need to ensure that all girls and boys get complete free, equitable and quality primary and secondary education. This is vital to lead them towards relevant and effective learning outcomes. b) It is also necessary to ensure that all girls and boys have access to quality early childhood development, care and pre-primary education so that they are ready for primary education. c) to provide equal access for all women and men to affordable and quality technical, vocational and tertiary education, including university, and d) to have a world where all youth and a substantial proportion of adults, both men and women, achieve literacy and numeracy.[225]

Jyotirao Phule had dedicated his life towards the emancipation of Indians who belong to the Shudra caste and worked tirelessly for the upliftment of women. He argued that in order to address social inequality, we must prioritize the education of women and the lower castes. For him, to throw open the gates of knowledge to women was the best way to emancipate Hindu women from their subjection to ancient beliefs and practices. His fight against tradition made him take a stance and struggle against the system of sati, child marriage and *kesha mundan*. He also firmly advocated for widow remarriage. For Phule, 'Knowledge advances the people, and the spread of female education will awaken the society.'[226]

Phule, along with his wife, Savitribai Phule, started their first school for girls in 1848 in Pune at Bhidewada. Unfortunately, Savitribai and Jyotirao Phule's success came with much resistance from the local community, which harboured conservative views. Savitribai often travelled to her school carrying an extra sari because she would be assailed by her conservative opposition with stones, dung and verbal abuse. However, the determination of these pioneers gave them the courage to face all adversities. In the 1850s, they were able to establish two educational trusts. These two trusts ended up encompassing many schools, which were then led by Savitribai Phule, and later, Fatima Sheikh.[227]

It is indeed a matter of pride that this unflinching drive towards women's empowerment has been witnessed all over India. The firm stance against child marriage led Ishwar Chandra Vidyasagar to strive to pass the Age of Consent Act of 1891. Even though widow remarriage was considered a flagrant breach of Hindu customs and was staunchly opposed by Bengali society of the time, Vidyasagar's efforts led Lord Dalhousie to personally finalize the bill and to the subsequent passing of the Hindu Widows' Remarriage Act in 1856.[228]

Perhaps one of the most important lessons that our study of such stalwarts of history unveils is the need for awareness. This awareness of equity and accessibility of education for all is pivotal. The need for a safe environment, which is absolutely essential for the realization of such a goal, is universal. What can we do as teachers to ensure that our students feel safe in our classrooms? Here are a few strategies we can use:

1. Build a Supportive Classroom Culture

Creating a supportive classroom culture is absolutely essential to enable students to thrive and develop. To build such a culture, a teacher can:

- Focus on developing positive relationships with students by showing an interest in their lives, empathizing with their concerns and getting to know them.

- Encourage a sense of community and collaboration among students by promoting group activities, respecting differences and opinions and encouraging students to work together as a team.
- Provide enough opportunities for students to express themselves without the fear of being judged.
- Celebrate student successes and acknowledge their efforts, even if they are small.
- Model positive behaviours and attitudes to set the tone for how students interact with each other and approach learning.

2. Address Bias and Stereotyping

This is crucial for creating an inclusive and equitable learning environment. Teachers can do this by examining their own biases and stereotypes, engaging in professional development to increase their cultural competence and modelling inclusive behaviour. Along with this, students need to be provided with opportunities to challenge and confront stereotypes. This can include exposing students to diverse perspectives and experiences, encouraging critical thinking and reflection and facilitating discussions around issues of bias and discrimination. Finally, teachers can encourage students to embrace and celebrate their own identities by promoting a positive self-image and appreciating the unique qualities and experiences of each student.

3. Promote Social and Emotional Learning

Social and emotional learning are essential for supporting student well-being.

- Teachers can teach social and emotional skills explicitly, such as self-awareness, empathy and responsible decision-making.
- They can provide opportunities for students to practise and apply these skills in real-world contexts, such as group projects or problem-solving scenarios.
- Teachers can use restorative practices to address conflicts and support positive behaviour, such as using mediation or reflection exercises to resolve conflicts and promote accountability.

Activities should not be used only for assessing learners but also to develop skills and to inculcate values. Interpersonal and life skills, such as seeing others' points of view, accepting responsibility, dealing with conflict and leadership qualities, must be developed through organizing various classroom and outdoor activities.[229]

Have you ever been overwhelmed with emotions as a child? Emotions like joy are easily identified, and more importantly, they do not usually disrupt our well-being. Whereas being scared, anxious, doubtful, among other emotions, play havoc in a child's life and often hamper their daily progress. But what if a child is unable to identify her/his feelings and is just demotivated? Here is a simple activity that teachers can use to help students identify what they are feeling and then work together to figure out a way ahead.

Create checkpoints with students on how they're doing emotionally. Students can be asked to take out time in the day or week for an 'emotions journal', where students can jot down any and all feelings they have had throughout the day or week. Teachers, with voluntary collaboration from the students, can then work on these journals and have heart-to-heart discussions. It is of immense importance that the teachers treat this exercise as significant and maintain the bond of trust that the student has entrusted her/him with.[230]

The NEP 2020 aims to instil ethics and human and constitutional values like empathy, respect for others, cleanliness, courtesy, democratic spirit, spirit of service, respect for public property, scientific temper, liberty, responsibility, pluralism, equality and justice in all students. Imparting life skills such as communication, cooperation, teamwork and resilience has also been prioritized.[231]

Let us now take a look at an activity that encourages students to think about moral values, and at the same time, helps teachers in imparting the concepts needed for the topic – the Indian Renaissance

Jar Full of Values.

Approximate duration: 10 minutes per student or groups of students.

Instructions and variations:

1. Teachers to write on small pieces of paper a few important values that students have learned through the study of the topic. Examples can be honesty, resilience, hard work, empathy, courage, etc.
2. Students can then be called individually or in groups to pick one value and prepare themselves as to what they can say or even come up with small skits to represent the chosen value as part of their learning of the given topic. The teachings of various leaders of the Indian Renaissance and how they have inspired the learners are the focus of this activity.

This can be a very effective method of formative assessment, practise of critical thinking, use of creativity and a good way of being rooted and proud of our country and its rich, diverse ancient and modern culture, knowledge systems and traditions.[232]

Accessibility

Marva Delores Collins was born in Alabama, USA, in 1936. She was a pioneer in offering high-quality education to children who might not have had access otherwise, making a lasting impression in the field of education.[233] Dismayed at the low levels of learning that she felt some students were experiencing in particular areas, Collins took around $5,000 from her own teacher's retirement fund and started a private school on the top floors of a brownstone in the West Garfield Park neighbourhood where she lived, in 1975. The school she started was called Westside Preparatory School. It soon became an educational and commercial success. Collins created her low-cost private school specifically for the purpose of teaching low-income children from the African-American community, whom Collins felt the Chicago Public School System had mislabelled as being 'learning disabled' . Collins stated that she had the data to prove that her students were teachable and were able to overcome obstacles of learning via her teaching methods, which she said eliminated behavioural issues and allowed students to flourish.

Collins felt that time spent with students was more valuable than creating audiovisual information that was used in classrooms. She and her daughter ran the school for more than 30 years, until it closed in 2008 due to a lack of sufficient enrolment and funding.

Marva Collins applied classical education, in particular the Socratic method, which she modified for use in primary schools and successfully with impoverished students. Collins criticized the way students were being taught and never the students who were in her classrooms. She wrote a number of manuals, books and motivational tracts describing her history and methods. In 1981, she was awarded the Jefferson Awards for Public Service – Award for Greatest Public Service Benefiting the Disadvantaged. In 2004, she became a National Humanities Medalist under the National Endowment for the Humanities.[234]

The next example of a champion for accessibility to education is from our own country.

Anand Kumar is an esteemed Indian mathematics educator known for his Super 30 programme, which was established in 2002 in Patna, Bihar. The programme aims to provide coaching to underprivileged students for the JEE-Main and JEE-Advanced entrance exams for the prestigious Indian Institutes of Technology (IITs). His programme has seen remarkable success, with numerous students, often from very humble backgrounds, gaining admission to the IITs. Kumar's contributions to education and literature were recognized with the Padma Shri award in 2023. And if this inspirational contribution of Kumar sounds very familiar to you, then there is a possibility that you have seen either or both of the following: the Discovery Channel documentary featuring Anand Kumar's work and the 2019 movie *Super 30*, with Hrithik Roshan playing the role of Kumar.[235]

Anand Kumar wants to make sure that young talents do not die out for lack of money. He started the Ramanujam School of Mathematics to provide inexpensive coaching and sponsor the higher education of needy children.[236]

Accountability

The NEP 2020 calls for a 'light but tight' regulatory framework for the country's education system to ensure integrity, transparency and resource efficiency. This is to be brought about through audit and public disclosure while encouraging innovation and out-of-the-box ideas through autonomy, good governance and empowerment. There is also a need for outstanding research to achieve outstanding education and development. A continuous and thorough review of progress based on sustained research and regular assessment by educational experts will keep the system updated and effective.[237]

The SDG4 aspires, by 2030, to substantially increase the supply of qualified teachers all over the world, including through international cooperation for teacher training in developing countries.[238] The NEP 2020 also puts teachers and faculty at the heart of the learning process. There is an emphasis on recruitment, continuous professional development, positive working environments and service conditions of teachers and educators in the country. The policy wants the education system to recognize, identify and foster the unique capabilities of each student by sensitizing teachers, as well as parents, to promote each student's holistic development in both academic and non-academic spheres. Learners to have the ability to choose their learning trajectories and programmes and thereby choose their own paths in life according to their talents and interests. For a more holistic education across different disciplines, the NEP 2020 urges teachers to focus on the basic unity and integrity of all knowledge.[239] In a multidisciplinary approach, each discipline works independently and contributes its expertise to a common goal. The focus here is problem-solving through contributions from various disciplines.[240] So, for example, a collaboration between the geography and mathematics departments on the use of linear regression to a geographical question that concerns links between income and population density will be considered as a multidisciplinary approach to teaching-learning. The most significant benefit here, then, is the likelihood of an increase in the student's overall confidence in both subjects![241]

An interdisciplinary approach involves a deeper level of integration, with disciplines working together to create a unified understanding of a complex issue. Interdisciplinary approaches often require more communication and cooperation between disciplines, leading to a more holistic and comprehensive understanding of the topic at hand.[242] In the recent past, when co-conducting a workshop for teachers and trainee teachers in Kolkata, I found the immense reach of interdisciplinary studies. The topic of discussion was 'Interdisciplinary Approach to Understand Perspectives', and the subjects involved were history – specific content being the genocide under the Nazis – and psychology – individual and situational debate. The result was an amazing discourse on how knowledge is both multiple (perspectives) and also at some level unified (concepts, contents, skills, etc).

Philosopher Karl Popper (1963) had famously observed,

'We are not students of some subject matter, but students of problems and problems may cut right across the boundaries of any subject matter or discipline.' Most real-life matters are multifaceted and have different types of causes and effects.[243] As a result, one of the major areas of emphasis in academia in recent years has been interdisciplinary research (studies), a trend that promises new insights and innovations that are rooted in cross-disciplinary collaboration. This required students to step beyond traditional disciplinary boundaries and apply knowledge and insights from multiple fields.[244]

Quality

The NEP 2020 has strongly emphasized that access to quality education must be considered a basic right of every child. Focus needs to be on conceptual understanding rather than rote learning and learning-for-exams. Creativity and 21st-century skills like critical thinking need to be encouraged. The education system in the country must strive towards logical decision-making and innovation.[245] The SDG4 points out that countries to ensure that all learners acquire the knowledge and skills needed to promote sustainable development. The key focus of education to include education for sustainable development and sustainable lifestyles, human rights, gender equality, promotion of a culture of peace and non-violence, global citizenship and appreciation of cultural diversity and of culture's contribution to sustainable development, and other topics.[246]

A discussion on the necessity of quality education needs an explanation of the famous Principles of Barak Rosenshine. An eminent educational researcher and professor of educational psychology, Rosenshine developed a set of teaching principles known as 'Rosenshine's Principles of Instruction'. These principles provide a bridge between educational research and classroom practices; thus, it is a step towards bringing in more research-based quality teaching practices, which leads to quality education. Rosenshine's principles are widely used in education worldwide, and each section includes details of the research finding underlying the principle and gives guidance on classroom practice.

Rosenshine's research draws from three main sources: research in cognitive science, research on the classroom practice of master teachers and research on cognitive support to help students learn complex tasks. In his 2012 article 'Principles of Instruction: Research-Based Strategies that All Teachers Should Know', Rosenshine described 10 research-based principles of instruction for teachers and educators:

1. A lesson to begin with a short review of prior learning.
2. New material to be presented in small steps with student practise after each step.
3. Teachers to ask a large number of questions and check the responses of all students.
4. Teachers to provide the model.
5. Teachers to guide practise done by students.

6. A regular check for student understanding is important.
7. Obtaining a high success rate in the classroom is vital.
8. Teachers to provide scaffolds for difficult tasks.
9. Teachers to call for and monitor independent practise by students.
10. Students need to be engaged in weekly and monthly reviews.

Let us now break down the above-mentioned principles to understand them in greater detail.

1. Daily review can strengthen previous learning and can lead to fluent recall: The review of previous learning can help us recall words, concepts and procedures effortlessly and automatically when we need this material to solve problems or to understand new material. The development of expertise requires thousands of hours of practise, and daily reviews is one component of this practice.

   After an experiment in an elementary school, it was found that teachers in the experiment were taught to spend eight minutes every day on review. Teachers used this time to check homework, go over problems where there were errors and practise the concepts and skills that needed to become automatic. As a result, students in these classrooms had higher achievement scores than did students in other classrooms.

   The most effective teachers in the studies of classroom instruction understood the importance of practise, and they began their lessons with a five-to-eight-minute review of previously covered material. It is important for a teacher to help students recall the concepts and vocabulary that will be relevant for the day's lesson because our working memory is very limited. If we do not review previous learning, then we will have to make a special effort to recall old material while learning new material, and this makes it difficult for us to learn the new material.

In addition, teachers might consider doing the following during their daily review:

- Correct homework.
- Review the concepts and skills that were practised as part of the homework.
- Ask students about points where they had difficulties or made errors.
- Review material where errors were made.
- Review material that needs overlearning (i.e., newly acquired skills should be practised well beyond the point of initial mastery, leading to automaticity).

The most effective teachers ensured that students efficiently acquired, rehearsed and connected knowledge. Many went on to hands-on activities but always after, not before, the basic material was learned.

2. Teacher to only present small amounts of new material at any time and then assist students as they practise this

material: Our working memory can only handle a few bits of information at once. Presenting too much material at once may confuse students because their working memory will be unable to process it. Therefore, the more effective teachers do not overwhelm their students by presenting too much new material at once. Rather, these teachers only present small amounts of new material at any time and then assist the students as they practise this material. Only after the students have mastered the first step do teachers proceed to the next step.

They checked their students' understanding on each point and retaught material when necessary. Some successful teachers taught by giving a series of short presentations, using many examples. The examples provided concrete learning and elaboration that were useful in processing new material. Teaching in small steps requires time, and the more effective teachers spent more time presenting new material and guiding student practise than did the less effective teachers.

In one study, the least effective teachers asked only nine questions in a 40-minute period. Compared with the successful teachers, the less effective teachers gave much shorter presentations and explanations and then passed out worksheets and told students to solve the problems. The less successful teachers were then observed going from student to student and having to explain the material again.

3. Questions help students practise new information and connect new material to their prior learning: Students need to practise new material. The teacher's questions and student discussions are a major way of providing this necessary practise. The most successful teachers in these studies spent more than half of the class time lecturing, demonstrating and asking questions. Questions allow a teacher to determine how well the material has been learned and whether there is a need for additional instruction. The most effective teachers also ask students to explain the process they used to answer the question – to explain how the answer was found. Less successful teachers ask fewer questions and almost no process questions.

   In one classroom-based experimental study, one group of teachers was taught to follow the presentation of new material with lots of questions. They were taught to increase the number of factual questions and process questions they asked during this guided practise. Test results showed that their students achieved higher scores than did students whose teachers did not receive the training. Imaginative teachers have found ways to involve all students in answering questions. Examples include having all students:

   - Tell the answer to a neighbour.
   - Summarize the main idea in one or two sentences, writing the summary on a piece of paper and sharing

this with a neighbour or repeating the procedure to a neighbour.

- Write the answer on a card and then hold it up.
- Raise their hands if they knew the answer (thereby allowing the teacher to check the entire class).
- Raise their hands if they agreed with the answer that someone else had given.

The following is a series of questions that teachers might ask when teaching literature, social science content or science content to their students. Sometimes, students may also develop questions from these stems to ask questions of each other

How are __________ and __________ alike?

What is the main idea of __________?

What are the strengths and weaknesses of __________?

In what way is __________ related to __________?

Compare __________ and __________ with regard to __________.

What do you think causes __________?

How does __________ tie in with what we have learned before?

Which one is the best __________, and why?

What are some possible solutions for the problem of __________?

Do you agree or disagree with this statement: __________?

What do you still not understand about __________?

4. Providing students with models and worked examples can help them learn to solve problems faster: Students need cognitive support to help them learn to solve problems. The teacher modelling and thinking aloud while demonstrating how to solve a problem are examples of effective cognitive support. Worked examples are another form of modelling that has been developed by researchers. Worked examples allow students to focus on the specific steps to solve problems and thus reduce the cognitive load on their working memory. Modelling and worked examples have been used successfully in mathematics, science, writing and reading comprehension. In a research carried out in Australia, students were given a mixture of problems to solve and worked examples. So, during independent practise, students first studied a worked example, then they solved a problem; then they studied another worked example and solved another problem. In this way, the worked examples showed students how to focus on the essential parts of the problems. Of course, not all students studied the worked examples. To correct this problem, the Australian researchers also presented partially completed problems in which students had to complete the missing steps and thus pay more attention to the worked example.

   Many of the skills taught in classrooms can be conveyed by providing prompts, modelling use of the prompt and then guiding students as they develop independence.

5. Successful teachers spend more time guiding students' practise of new material: An important finding from information-processing research is that students need to spend additional time rephrasing, elaborating and summarizing new material in order to store this material in their long-term memory. When there has been sufficient rehearsal, the students are able to retrieve this material easily and thus are able to make use of this material to foster new learning and aid in problem-solving. But when the rehearsal time is too short, students are less able to store, remember or use the material. As we know, it is relatively easy to place something in a filing cabinet, but it can be very difficult to recall where exactly we filed it. Rehearsal helps us remember where we filed it so we can access it with ease when needed.

   Teachers who spent more time in guided practise and had higher success rates also had students who were more engaged during individual work at their desks. This finding suggests that when teachers provided sufficient instruction during guided practise, the students were better prepared for the independent practice (e.g., seatwork and homework activities), but when the guided practise was too short, the students were not prepared for the seatwork and made more errors during independent practise.

A teacher can facilitate this rehearsal process by asking questions; good questions require students to process and rehearse the material. Rehearsal is also enhanced when students are asked to summarize the main points and when they are supervised as they practise new steps in a skill. The quality of storage in long-term memory will be weak if students only skim the material and do not engage with it. It is also important that all students process the new material and receive feedback so that they do not inadvertently store partial information or a misconception in long-term memory.

6. Checking for student understanding at each point can help students learn the material with fewer errors: The more effective teachers frequently checked to see if all the students were learning the new material. These checks provided some of the processing needed to move new learning into long-term memory. These checks also let teachers know if students were developing misconceptions.

   Effective teachers also stopped to check for student understanding. They checked for understanding by asking questions, by asking students to summarize the presentation up to that point or to repeat directions or procedures or by asking students whether they agreed or disagreed with other students' answers. Another way to check for understanding is to ask students to think aloud as they work to solve mathematical problems, plan an essay or identify the main idea in a paragraph. Yet another check is to ask students to explain or defend their position to others. Having to explain a position may help students integrate and elaborate their knowledge in new ways or may help identify gaps in their understanding. In contrast, the less effective teachers simply asked, 'Are there any questions?' and if there were no questions, they assumed the students had learned the material and proceeded to pass out worksheets for students to complete on their own.

7. It is important for students to achieve a high success rate during classroom instruction: In two major studies on the impact of teachers, the investigators found that students in classrooms with more effective teachers had a higher success rate, as judged by the quality of their oral responses during guided practise and their individual work. A high success rate during guided practise also leads to a higher success rate when students are working on problems on their own. The research also suggests that the optimal success rate for fostering student achievement appears to be about 80 per cent. A success rate of 80 per cent shows that students are learning the material, and it also shows that the students are challenged.

   I once observed a class where an effective teacher was going from desk to desk during independent practise and suddenly realized that the students were having difficulty. She stopped the work, told the students not to do the problems for homework and said she would reteach the material the next day. She stopped the work because she did not want the students to practise errors. Unless all students have mastered the first set of lessons, there is a danger that the slower students will fall further behind when the next set of lessons is taught. So there is a need for a high success rate for all students. 'Mastery learning' is a form of instruction where lessons are organized into short units and all the students are required to master one set of lessons before they proceed to the next set. In mastery learning, tutoring by other students or by teachers is provided to help students master each unit. Variations of this approach, particularly the tutoring, might be useful in many classroom settings.

8. The teacher provides students with temporary supports and scaffolds to assist them when they learn difficult tasks: Scaffolds include modelling the steps by the teacher or thinking aloud by the teacher as he/she solves the problem. Scaffolds also may be tools, such as cue cards or checklists, that complete part of the task for the students or a model of the completed task against which students can compare their own work. The process of helping students solve difficult problems by modelling and providing scaffolds is called 'cognitive apprenticeship'. Students learn strategies and

content during this apprenticeship, which enable them to become competent readers, writers and problem-solvers. They are aided by a master who models, coaches, provides supports and scaffolds them as they become independent.

Similarly, one researcher developed the following prompt to help students organize material. 1. Draw a central box and write the title of the article in it. 2. Skim the article to find four to six main ideas. 3. Write each main idea in a box below the central box. 4. Find and write two to four important details to list under each main idea.

In some of the studies, students were given a checklist to evaluate their work. Checklist items included 'Have I found the most important information that tells me more about the main idea?' and 'Does every sentence start with a capital letter?' The teacher then modelled the use of the checklist.

9. Students need extensive, successful, independent practise for skills and knowledge to become automatic: This independent practise is necessary because a good deal of practise (overlearning) is needed to become fluent and automatic in a skill. When material is overlearned, it can be recalled automatically and doesn't take up any space in working memory. When students become automatic in an area, they can then devote more of their attention to comprehension and application.

Independent practise provides students with the additional review and elaboration they need to become fluent. This need for fluency applies to facts, concepts and discriminations that must be used in subsequent learning.

The more successful teachers provided for extensive and successful practise, both in the classroom and after class. Independent practise should involve the same material as the guided practise. Research has found that students were more engaged when their teacher circulated around the room and monitored and supervised their seatwork. The optimal time for these contacts was 30 seconds or less. Classrooms where the teachers had to stop at students' desks and provide a great deal of explanation during seatwork were the classrooms where students were making errors. These errors occurred because the guided practise was not sufficient for students to engage productively in independent practise. This reiterates the importance of adequately preparing students before they begin their independent practise.

Some investigators have developed procedures, such as cooperative learning, during which students help each other as they study. Research has shown that all students tend to achieve more in these settings than do students in regular settings. Presumably, some of the advantage comes from having to explain the material to someone else and/or having someone else (other than the teacher) explain the material to the student. Cooperative learning offers an opportunity for students to get feedback from their peers about correct, as well as incorrect responses, which promotes both engagement and learning.

10. Students need to be involved in extensive practise to develop well-connected and automatic knowledge: The best way to become an expert is through practise – thousands of hours of practise. The more the practise, the better the performance.

    The more one rehearses and reviews information, the stronger these interconnections become. It is also easier to solve new problems when one has a rich, well-connected body of knowledge and strong ties among the connections. One of the goals of education is to help students develop extensive and available background knowledge. Knowledge (even very extensive knowledge) stored in long-term memory that is organized into patterns only occupies a tiny amount of space in our limited working memory. So, having larger and better-connected patterns of knowledge frees up space in our working memory. This available space can be used for reflecting on new information and for problem-solving. The development of well-connected patterns (also called 'unitization' and 'chunking') and the freeing of space in the working memory are hallmarks of an expert in a field. Thus, research on cognitive processing supports the need for a teacher to assist students by providing for extensive reading of a variety of materials, frequent reviews and discussion and application activities. The research on cognitive processing suggests that these classroom activities help students increase the number of pieces of information in their long-term memory and organize this information into patterns and chunks. The more one rehearses and reviews information, the stronger the interconnections between the materials become. Review also helps students to develop their new knowledge into patterns, and it helps them acquire the ability to recall past learning automatically.

Teachers face a difficult problem when they need to cover a lot of material and don't feel they have the time for sufficient review. But the research states (and we all know from personal experience) that material that is not adequately practised and reviewed is easily forgotten.

Notes

1. A.P.J. Abdul Kalam, *Turning Points*, 8.
2. https://egyankosh.ac.in/bitstream/123456789/46000/1/Unit-1.pdf
3. https://www.jstor.org/stable/41303487, p 57
4. https://www.jstor.org/stable/41303487, pp58-59
5. https://www.oxfordbibliographies.com/display/document/obo-9780195389661/obo-9780195389661-0328.xml#:~:text=The%20Theaetetus%20along%20with%20the%20Meno%20and%20Republic,for%20understanding%20Plato%E2%80%99s%20epistemology%20and%20theory%20of%20knowledge.
6. https://www.britannica.com/topic/The-Republic
7. https://www.oxfordbibliographies.com/display/document/obo-9780195389661/obo-9780195389661-0328.xml#:~:text=The%20Theaetetus%20along%20with%20the%20Meno%20and%20Republic,for%20understanding%20Plato%E2%80%99s%20epistemology%20and%20theory%20of%20knowledge.
8. https://egyankosh.ac.in/bitstream/123456789/45999/1/Unit-2.pdf
9. https://www.jstor.org/stable/23715723, p4
10. https://www.jstor.org/stable/23715723, p4
11. https://www.jstor.org/stable/20866923 p 757
12. Suchita Mondal, *Pedagogy of Social Sciences Teaching*, 13.
13. https://oxfordre.com/literature/display/10.1093/acrefore/9780190201098.001.0001/acrefore-9780190201098-e-1032
14. https://oxfordre.com/literature/display/10.1093/acrefore/9780190201098.001.0001/acrefore-9780190201098-e-1032

15. NEP 2020, 3.
16. Suchita Mondal, *Pedagogy of Social Sciences Teaching*, p 14.
17. Suchita Mondal, *Pedagogy of Social Sciences Teaching*, p 14
18. https://www.educationcorner.com/learning-theories-in-education/
19. https://www.growthengineering.co.uk/learning-theories/
20. https://www.educationcorner.com/learning-theories-in-education/
21. https://www.educationcorner.com/learning-theories-in-education/
22. https://www.educationcorner.com/learning-theories-in-education/
23. https://www.educationcorner.com/learning-theories-in-education/
24. https://www.growthengineering.co.uk/learning-theories/
25. By Silly rabbit - self-made (by User:Silly rabbit). Updated in the Gimp by User:Michaelrayw2., CC BY 3.0, https://commons.wikimedia.org/w/index.php?curid=115478248
26. Unknown (pre-1923 photo). Watson, as per the link in the source, left Johns Hopkins in 1921 (on bad terms). This is a photo of him there. http://www.jhu.edu/gazette/2001/jan2201/22watson.html The Johns Hopkins Gazette (Johns Hopkins University), Public Domain, https://commons.wikimedia.org/w/index.php?curid=21212553
27. Unknown author. http://ihm.nlm.nih.gov/images/B21072, Public Domain, https://commons.wikimedia.org/w/index.php?curid=19270394
28. https://neurolaunch.com/reward-system-for-child-behaviour/
29. https://www.growthengineering.co.uk/gamification-badges-lms/
30. https://www.growthengineering.co.uk/behavioural-learning-theory/
31. https://www.growthengineering.co.uk/behavioural-learning-theory/
32. https://www.growthengineering.co.uk/behavioural-learning-theory/
33. https://en.wikipedia.org/wiki/Stanley_Ka_Dabba

34. https://www.growthengineering.co.uk/behavioural-learning-theory/
35. https://www.growthengineering.co.uk/behavioural-learning-theory/
36. principles_for_effective_pedagogy_QuickStart.pdf (ncrm.ac.uk)
37. https://elearningindustry.com/what-is-gamification-and-how-does-it-work
38. https://www.simplypsychology.org/bandura.html
39. https://www.firstcry.com/intelli/articles/monkey-and-the-cap-seller-story-with-moral-for-kids/
40. https://en.wikipedia.org/wiki/Social_learning_theory
41. https://en.wikipedia.org/wiki/Social_learning_theory
42. https://en.wikipedia.org/wiki/Social_learning_theory
43. https://helpfulprofessor.com/learning-theories/
44. Albert Bandura, original publication: Bandura's local photo-developing store. Immediate source: https://btr.mt, Fair use, https://en.wikipedia.org/w/index.php?curid=60909577
45. https://helpfulprofessor.com/learning-theories/
46. https://en.wikipedia.org/wiki/Experiential_learning
47. https://experientiallearninginstitute.org/what-is-experiential-learning/
48. https://cisce.org/wp-content/uploads/2022/10/History-and-Civics-at-Upper-Primary-Level.pdf
49. https://ncf.ncert.gov.in/webadmin/assets/b27f04eb-65af-467f-af12-105275251546
50. https://eprints.ncrm.ac.uk/id/eprint/3766/1/principles_for_effective_pedagogy_QuickStart.pdf
51. https://cisce.org/wp-content/uploads/2022/10/History-and-Civics-at-Upper-Primary-Level.pdf
52. https://ncf.ncert.gov.in/webadmin/assets/b27f04eb-65af-467f-af12-105275251546
53. https://en.wikipedia.org/wiki/Interview
54. https://lf.westernsydney.edu.au/engage/strategy/panel-discussions/
55. https://en.wikipedia.org/wiki/Miss_Marple

56. https://en.wikipedia.org/wiki/Sherlock_Holmes
57. https://en.wikipedia.org/wiki/Feluda
58. https://en.wikipedia.org/wiki/Feluda
59. https://dictionary.cambridge.org/dictionary/english/cognition
60. https://en.wikipedia.org/wiki/Cognition
61. https://en.wikipedia.org/wiki/Cognitivism_(psychology)
62. By After Frans Hals - André Hatala [e.a.] (1997) De eeuw van Rembrandt, Bruxelles: Crédit communal de Belgique, ISBN 2-908388-32-4., Public Domain, https://commons.wikimedia.org/w/index.php?curid=2774313
63. https://en.wikipedia.org/wiki/Ren%C3%A9_Descartes
64. https://en.wikipedia.org/wiki/Cogito,_ergo_sum
65. https://www.growthengineering.co.uk/cognitive-learning-theory/
66. https://www.growthengineering.co.uk/learning-theories/
67. https://www.growthengineering.co.uk/cognitive-learning-theory/
68. https://www.growthengineering.co.uk/learning-theories/
69. https://www.growthengineering.co.uk/cognitive-learning-theory/
70. https://en.wikipedia.org/wiki/Jean_Piaget
71. Unidentified (Ensian published by the University of Michigan), 1968 Michiganensian, 91, Public Domain, https://commons.wikimedia.org/w/index.php?curid=53878611
72. https://www.growthengineering.co.uk/cognitive-learning-theory/
73. https://www.growthengineering.co.uk/cognitive-learning-theory/
74. https://www.growthengineering.co.uk/cognitive-learning-theory/
75. https://www.educationcorner.com/learning-theories-in-education/
76. https://en.wikipedia.org/wiki/Gestalt_psychology
77. https://www.educationcorner.com/learning-theories-in-education/
78. https://en.wikipedia.org/wiki/Gestalt_psychology
79. https://en.wikipedia.org/wiki/Structuralism_(psychology)
80. https://helpfulprofessor.com/structuralism-in-psychology/

81. https://www.educationcorner.com/learning-theories-in-education/
82. https://www.educationcorner.com/learning-theories-in-education/
83. https://www.theanimatedteacherblog.com/pedagogical-strategies-for-teaching/
84. https://www.educationcorner.com/cognitive-load-theory/
85. https://www.theanimatedteacherblog.com/pedagogical-strategies-for-teaching/
86. https://www.educationcorner.com/cognitive-load-theory/
87. https://www.theanimatedteacherblog.com/pedagogical-strategies-for-teaching/
88. https://www.educationcorner.com/cognitive-load-theory/
89. https://www.theanimatedteacherblog.com/pedagogical-strategies-for-teaching/
90. https://www.educationcorner.com/cognitive-load-theory/
91. https://www.educationcorner.com/cognitive-load-theory/
92. https://www.theanimatedteacherblog.com/pedagogical-strategies-for-teaching/
93. https://www.theanimatedteacherblog.com/pedagogical-strategies-for-teaching/
94. https://www.facinghistory.org/resource-library/fishbowl
95. https://www.theedadvocate.org/how-to-implement-the-fishbowl-teaching-strategy-in-your-classroom/
96. https://teachandgo.com/good-debate-topics-students/
97. https://www.theedadvocate.org/how-to-implement-the-fishbowl-teaching-strategy-in-your-classroom/
98. https://files.eric.ed.gov/fulltext/EJ1086242.pdf
99. https://vajiramandravi.com/quest-upsc-notes/decline-of-indus-valley-civilization/
100. https://www.theanimatedteacherblog.com/pedagogical-strategies-for-teaching/
101. https://chatgpt.com/
102. https://chatgpt.com/
103. https://www.theanimatedteacherblog.com/pedagogical-strategies-for-teaching/

104. *Rosenshine's principles.pdf
105. https://ncf.ncert.gov.in/webadmin/assets/b27f04eb-65af-467f-af12-105275251546
106. https://www.teachermagazine.com/au_en/articles/classroom-teaching-techniques-socratic-circles
107. https://zonofeducation.com/socratic-method-of-teaching/
108. https://www.theanimatedteacherblog.com/pedagogical-strategies-for-teaching/
109. https://en.wikipedia.org/wiki/Robert_M._Gagn%C3%A9
110. https://en.wikipedia.org/wiki/Robert_M._Gagn%C3%A9
111. https://www.theanimatedteacherblog.com/pedagogical-strategies-for-teaching/
112. https://www.theanimatedteacherblog.com/pedagogical-strategies-for-teaching/
113. https://en.wikipedia.org/wiki/Robert_M._Gagn%C3%A9#cite_note-12
114. https://www.jstor.org/stable/40364708
115. https://www.theanimatedteacherblog.com/pedagogical-strategies-for-teaching/
116. https://www.jstor.org/stable/40364708
117. https://en.wikipedia.org/wiki/David_Ausubel
118. https://en.wikipedia.org/wiki/Deductive_reasoning
119. https://files.eric.ed.gov/fulltext/EJ1165490.pdf, page 1
120. https://files.eric.ed.gov/fulltext/EJ1165490.pdf, page 6
Picture on mind map pattern 2 https://en.wikipedia.org/wiki/Indian_Rebellion_of_1857#/media/File:The_Sepoy_revolt_at_Meerut.jpg
121. https://paperperk.com/blog/how-to-write-a-book-review
122. https://paperperk.com/blog/how-to-write-a-book-review
123. https://paperperk.com/blog/how-to-write-a-book-review
124. https://www.theanimatedteacherblog.com/pedagogical-strategies-for-teaching/
125. https://en.wikipedia.org/wiki/Family_tree
126. https://en.wikipedia.org/wiki/Tree_structure

127. https://en.wikipedia.org/wiki/David_Ausubel
128. https://www.ndtv.com/india-news/viral-interview-zakir-hussain-on-having-rhythms-for-prayers-from-father-7257633
129. https://thepersonage.com/wp-content/uploads/2020/07/Zakir-Hussain-Musician-Images.jpg
130. https://en.wikipedia.org/wiki/Serena_Williams#Early_life
131. https://thetennisbros.com/tennis-tips/tactics/tennis-singles-strategy/
132. https://en.wikipedia.org/wiki/Theory_of_multiple_intelligences
133. https://www.theanimatedteacherblog.com/pedagogical-strategies-for-teaching/
134. https://ctl.stanford.edu/differentiated-instruction
135. https://cisce.org/wp-content/uploads/2022/10/History-and-Civics-at-Upper-Primary-Level.pdf
136. https://www.suraasa.com/blog/lecture-method
137. https://www.weareteachers.com/25-formative-assessment-options/
138. https://en.wikipedia.org/wiki/Buddhist_architecture#/media/File:Sanchi1_N-MP-220.jpg
139. https://en.wikipedia.org/wiki/Buddhist_architecture#/media/File:Ajanta_Caves,_India,_Ajanta_stupa_worship_hall.jpg
140. https://en.wikipedia.org/wiki/Jain_temple#/media/File:Delwada.jpg
141. https://www.edglossary.org/exhibition/#:~:text=In%20education%2C%20the%20term%20exhibition%20refers%20to%20projects%2C,have%20achieved%20expected%20learning%20standards%20or%20learning%20objectives.
142. https://helpfulprofessor.com/learning-theories/.
143. https://opentext.wsu.edu/theoreticalmodelsforteachingandresearch/chapter/multimedia-learning-theory/#:~:text=Multimedia%20Learning%20Theory%20%28MMLT%29%20was%20originally%20developed%20by,three%20aspects%20that%20help%20students%20learn%20more%20effectively.

144. History-and-Civics-at-Upper-Primary-Level.pdf (cisce.org)
145. b27f04eb-65af-467f-af12-105275251546 (ncert.gov.in)
146. https://oar.marine.ie/bitstream/handle/10793/929/Lesson Plan_Art_Save%20the%20Seas%203D%20Poster_171213.pdf?sequence=1&isAllowed=y
147 https://www.researchgate.net/publication/326356212_METHODS_AND_RESOURCES_IN_TEACHING_SOCIAL_STUDIES
148. https://www.verywellmind.com/verbal-linguistic-intelligence-8643191
149 https://www.researchgate.net/publication/282867557_USING_EXTEMPORE_AS_A_TASK_TO_IMPROVE_ORAL_COMMUNICATION_SKILLS
150. https://www.esldebates.com/80-debating-topics-on-the-environment/
151. https://psychologyfor.com/interpersonal-intelligence-what-it-is-examples-and-activities-to-improve-it/
152. https://aftonvilla.com/the-benefits-of-a-plantation-drive/
153. https://www.globalcitizen.org/en/content/why-planting-trees-helps-fight-climate-change/
154. https://www.verywellmind.com/what-is-active-listening-3024343
155. https://www.simplypsychology.org/active-listening-definition-skills-benefits.html
156. https://www.masterclass.com/articles/how-to-build-music-listening-skills
157. https://en.wikipedia.org/wiki/Reetigowla
158. https://en.wikipedia.org/wiki/Brindavani_Sarang
159. https://hbr.org/2024/01/what-is-active-listening
160. https://hbr.org/2024/01/what-is-active-listening
161. https://hbr.org/2024/01/what-is-active-listening
162. https://scottjeffrey.com/intrapersonal-intelligence/

163. https://www.theedadvocate.org/understanding-intrapersonal-intelligence/
164. https://en.wikipedia.org/wiki/Critical_thinking
165. Underwood & Underwood. This image is available from the United States Library of Congress's Prints and Photographs division under the digital ID cph.3a51565. This tag does not indicate the copyright status of the attached work. A normal copyright tag is still required. See Commons: Licensing., Public Domain, https://commons.wikimedia.org/w/index.php?curid=43191685
166. https://www.psychmechanics.com/why-intrapersonal-intelligence-matters/
167. https://www.coursera.org/articles/critical-thinking-skills
168. NEP 2020, 5.
169. https://www.weareteachers.com/types-of-assessments/
170. https://www.health.harvard.edu/blog/the-thinking-benefits-of-doodling-2016121510844
171. https://www.weareteachers.com/25-formative-assessment-options/
172. https://www.modelteaching.com/education-articles/teaching-strategies/the-four-corners-strategy-a-verbal-active-method-to-check-for-understanding
173. https://cisce.org/wp-content/uploads/2022/10/History-and-Civics-at-Upper-Primary-Level.pdf
174. https://helpfulprofessor.com/learning-theories/
175. Androidmarsexpress: Own work, CC BY-SA 4.0, https://commons.wikimedia.org/w/index.php?curid=93026655
176. By http://www.celebriton.com/abraham_maslow/photo/a_photo_of_abraham_maslow, Fair use, https://en.wikipedia.org/w/index.php?curid=34062949
177. https://helpfulprofessor.com/learning-theories/
178. https://cisce.org/wp-content/uploads/2022/10/History-and-Civics-at-Upper-Primary-Level.pdf

179. https://en.wikipedia.org/wiki/Blind_men_and_an_elephant
180. https://www.educationcorner.com/learning-theories-in-education/
181. https://en.wikipedia.org/wiki/Blind_men_and_an_elephant
182. https://www.educationcorner.com/learning-theories-in-education/
183. https://www.educationcorner.com/learning-theories-in-education/
184. https://helpfulprofessor.com/spiral-curriculum/
185. https://www.francisbriers.com/blog/2010/8/16/3-cultural-learning-styles-linear-cyclical-and-holistic.html
186. https://helpfulprofessor.com/spiral-curriculum/
187. https://www.britannica.com/science/taxonomy
188. https://en.wikipedia.org/wiki/Bloom%27s_taxonomy
189. https://helpfulprofessor.com/spiral-curriculum/
190. https://helpfulprofessor.com/spiral-curriculum/
191. https://www.anu.edu.au/students/academic-skills/writing-assessment/report-writing#:~:text=A%20report%20is%20a%20specific,coming%20up%20with%20a%20solution.
192. https://www.ncbi.nlm.nih.gov/pmc/articles/PMC3612296/
193. https://www.ncbi.nlm.nih.gov/pmc/articles/PMC3612296/
194. https://www.rasmussen.edu/degrees/education/blog/types-of-learning-styles/
195. https://vark-learn.com/introduction-to-vark/the-vark-modalities/
196. https://www.masterclass.com/articles/what-is-a-podcast
197. https://www.masterclass.com/articles/what-is-a-podcast
198. https://www.bbcearth.com/podcast
199. https://www.rasmussen.edu/degrees/education/blog/types-of-learning-styles/
200. https://www.masterclass.com/articles/what-is-a-podcast
201. https://en.wikipedia.org/wiki/Pop_filter
202. https://www.masterclass.com/articles/what-is-a-podcast
203. https://en.wikipedia.org/wiki/Psychomotor_learning
204. https://www.researchgate.net/publication/360412639_DRAMA_EDUCATION_A_NEED_FOR_THE_HOLISTIC_GROWTH_OF_THE_LEARNERS
205. https://nandikar.net/about-us/

206. https://timesofindia.indiatimes.com/city/kolkata/Stress-buster-Drama-may-be-part-of-school-curriculum/articleshow/5709909.cms
207. https://www.researchgate.net/publication/326356212_METHODS_AND_RESOURCES_IN_TEACHING_SOCIAL_STUDIES
208. https://www.rasmussen.edu/degrees/education/blog/types-of-learning-styles/
209. https://www.rasmussen.edu/degrees/education/blog/types-of-learning-styles/
210. https://files.eric.ed.gov/fulltext/EJ1165490.pdf, page 1
211. https://files.eric.ed.gov/fulltext/EJ1165490.pdf , page 6
Picture on mind map pattern 2: https://en.wikipedia.org/wiki/Indian_Rebellion_of_1857#/media/File:The_Sepoy_revolt_at_Meerut.jpg
212. https://helpfulprofessor.com/learning-theories/
213. https://journals.sagepub.com/doi/full/10.1111/j.1539-6053.2009.01038.x
214. https://helpfulprofessor.com/learning-theories/
215. https://www.cast.org/about/about-cast
216. https://udlguidelines.cast.org/
217. https://www.rasmussen.edu/degrees/education/blog/types-of-learning-styles/
218. https://sdgs.un.org/2030agenda
219. https://www.education.gov.in/nep/about-nep
220. https://www.education.gov.in/nep/about-nep
221. https://www.education.gov.in/nep/about-nep
222. https://www.education.gov.in/sites/upload_files/mhrd/files/NEP_Final_English_0.pdf
223. https://sdgs.un.org/2030agenda
224. https://www.education.gov.in/sites/upload_files/mhrd/files/NEP_Final_English_0.pdf

225. https://sdgs.un.org/2030agenda
226. Mugali, Shiladhar Yallappa and Priyadarshini Sharanappa Amadihal. 'MAHATMA JYOTIRAO PHULE'S VIEWS ON UPLIFTMENT OF WOMEN AS REFLECTED IN SARVAJANIK STAYADHARMA', *Proceedings of the Indian History Congress*, vol. 69, 2008, 691–700. *JSTOR*, http://www.jstor.org/stable/44147232. Accessed 20 Apr. 2025.
227. https://en.wikipedia.org/wiki/Savitribai_Phule
228. https://en.wikipedia.org/wiki/Ishwar_Chandra_Vidyasagar
229. https://cisce.org/wp-content/uploads/2022/10/History-and-Civics-at-Upper-Primary-Level.pdf
230. https://growingleaders.com/the-importance-of-sensitivity-in-your-students-empathy-skills/
231. https://www.education.gov.in/sites/upload_files/mhrd/files/NEP_Final_English_0.pdf
232. https://www.education.gov.in/sites/upload_files/mhrd/files/NEP_Final_English_0.pdf
233. https://www.thefamouspeople.com/educators.php
234. https://www.thefamouspeople.com/educators.php
235. https://www.thefamouspeople.com/educators.php
236. https://www.thefamouspeople.com/educators.php
237. https://www.education.gov.in/sites/upload_files/mhrd/files/NEP_Final_English_0.pdf
238. https://sdgs.un.org/2030agenda
239. https://www.education.gov.in/sites/upload_files/mhrd/files/NEP_Final_English_0.pdf
240. https://thisvsthat.io/interdisciplinary-vs-multidisciplinary
241. https://files.eric.ed.gov/fulltext/EJ1329010.pdf
242. https://thisvsthat.io/interdisciplinary-vs-multidisciplinary
243. https://www.researchgate.net/publication/331689047_An_introduction_to_interdisciplinary_research
244. https://www.researchgate.net/publication/331689047_An_introduction_to_interdisciplinary_research, page 13

245. https://www.education.gov.in/sites/upload_files/mhrd/files/NEP_Final_English_0.pdf
246. https://sdgs.un.org/2030agenda

Image Copyright Information

1. **B.F. Skinner** – Silly rabbit, CC BY 3.0 <https://creativecommons.org/licenses/by/3.0>, via Wikimedia Commons
2. **John B. Watson** – Unknown (pre-1923 photo) Watson, per the link in the source, left Johns Hopkins in 1921 (on bad terms). This is a photo of him there., Public domain, via Wikimedia Commons
3. **Ivan Pavlov** – http://ihm.nlm.nih.gov/images/B21072, Public domain, via Wikimedia Commons
4. **Design of badges for highest scores** – Created by MetaAI
5. **Bandura's Bobodoll experiment** – Usman Zafar Paracha/Shutterstock.com
6. **Satyajit Ray** – Dinu Alam Newyork, CC BY-SA 4.0 <https://creativecommons.org/licenses/by-sa/4.0>, via Wikimedia Commons
7. **Rene Descartes** – After Frans Hals, Public domain, via Wikimedia Commons
8. **Jean Piaget** – Unidentified (Ensian published by University of Michigan), Public domain, via Wikimedia Commons

9. **Ustad Zakir Hussain** – Krupasindhu Muduli, CC BY-SA 3.0 <https://creativecommons.org/licenses/by-sa/3.0>, via Wikimedia Commons
10. **Sanchi Stupa** – deepak bishnoi/Shutterstock.com
11. **A Chaitya in Ajanta Caves** – Dey.sandip, CC BY-SA 3.0 <https://creativecommons.org/licenses/by-sa/3.0>, via Wikimedia Commons
12. **Jain Temple, Dilwara** – Malaiya at en.wikipedia, GFDL <http://www.gnu.org/copyleft/fdl.html>, via Wikimedia Commons
13. **John Dewey** – Underwood & Underwood, Public domain, via Wikimedia Commons
14. **Maslow's Hierarchy of Needs** – alinabel/Shutterstock.com
15. **Jyotirao Phule** – Internet, CC0, via Wikimedia Commons